Implementing and Improving Teaming:
A Handbook for Middle Level Leaders

NEW ENLARGED EDITION

Jerry Rottier

National Middle School Association
Westerville, Ohio

National Middle School Association
4151 Executive Parkway
Suite 300
Westerville, Ohio 43081
Telephone (800) 528-NMSA

Printed in the United States of America.

Fourth Printing, January 2005

Sue Swaim, Executive Director
Jeff Ward, Deputy Executive Director
April Tibbles, Director of Publications
Edward Brazee, Editor, Professional Publications
John Lounsbury, Consulting Editor, Professional Publications
Mary Mitchell, Designer and Editorial Assistant
Marcia Meade-Hurst, Senior Publications Representative

Library of Congress Cataloging-in-Publication Data

Rottier, Jerry
    Implementing and improving teaming: a handbook for middle level leaders/by Jerry Rottier.-- New enlarged ed.
        p. cm.
    Includes bibliographical references
    ISBN: 1-56090-166-7
    1. Teaching teams--United States--Handbooks, manuals, etc. 2. Middle schools--United States--Handbooks, manuals, etc. I. Title.

LB1029.T4 R68 2001
373.14'8--dc21   00-067877

Contents

About the Author

Jerry Rottier, a charter member of the National Middle School Association, has been active in middle level education throughout the United States presenting at conferences, providing workshops, and consulting with school districts. For many years he taught graduate and undergraduate courses in middle level education at the University of Wisconsin-Eau Claire. Dr. Rottier has written numerous articles on middle level issues and co-authored a book on cooperative learning. He also directs the Center for Middle Level Assessment which provides assessment instruments to middle level schools.

Dedication

To my teammate of many years, Lois, for her support in my work in middle level education. Thank you!

Acknowledgement

Special appreciation is extended to Kim Rottier for the original artwork.

Foreword: Achieving Unrealized Potential

Interdisciplinary teams continue to be the most distinguishing feature of modern middle schools, and their advocacy has not waned over the last three decades. However, behind the now common organizational presence of teams exists a widely recognized failure to exploit the powerful potential of teaming.

Teachers all too often have not heeded sufficiently the admonition of Henry David Thoreau who warned, "Beware of enterprises that require new clothes, but not rather a new wearer of clothes." Although readily accepting assignments as members of an interdisciplinary team and using common planning time for much collaboration on managerial matters, too many teachers put on the clothes of teaming but continued to teach essentially as they taught before when they were single runners.

Perhaps we thought naïvely that teams once formed would understand the value of teaming and move to put into practice instructional and curriculum strategies that teaming makes possible. But, with limited exceptions, such has not proven to be the case. Teams became symbolic evidences of desired change but did not assure change in the way classrooms were conducted. Long-standing habits and assumptions about accepted ways to teach simply held sway. This is, of course, understandable, given the pressure-packed work of classroom teachers. Teaming, not a part of most teachers' experiences either when they were students or in earlier teaching, remains, therefore, something of a vague vision. The skills and nuances needed to make teaming work effectively simply are not present in their repertoires, and the time to achieve them is in short supply. Teams remain in many teachers' views as ends not as means. With rare exceptions, it is true that teachers like being on teams and recognize many obvious benefits; but they seldom tap the possibilities for making the major changes in the teaching-learning enterprise that will lead to significantly improved students' overall education and academic achievement.

The idea of doing your own work is deeply ingrained in the culture of the school and in our society. Yet research and cumulative experience have demonstrated that teamwork pays off – in business, in the military, in families and communities, and, of course, in schools. Teams simply can achieve results well beyond what individuals working by themselves can accomplish. The success of cooperative learning is a testament to the validity of this truth. As Jimmy Durante used to say, "Everybody knows more than anybody." Teaming should never be abandoned because of its cost, as has sometimes been done; rather, it should be revitalized so that its potential for increased student achievement can be realized.

This new resource will go a long way to help teams become more aware of teaming's possibilities and provide many specific suggestions for taking the disciplined action that is necessary for teams to be all they could be. This new edition, with more eye-catching drawings, includes most of the material contained in the very successful original edition; however, it has been substantially enlarged and updated. This volume will have immediate value on a first reading, but it provides much more, for it is a resource that teams will return to regularly as they continue their journey on the sometimes rocky road that leads to the full implementation of the middle school concept.

— John H. Lounsbury

Introduction

Teaming has become the dominant organizational pattern in middle level schools. The complexity of demands made on schools and the curriculum simply does not support the one teacher/one group of students/one subject model. Teams of teachers, sharing their knowledge, skills, and philosophies have become the organizational model that leads our schools in the new century. While some middle schools still need assistance in the initial implementation of teaming, more need to reflect on their current practices and make changes in order to achieve the full benefits of teaming. Based on extensive experiences with teaming, we know what teaming practices produce positive results. With this knowledge, we have no excuse for not making teaming as effective and efficient as possible.

Implementing and Improving Teaming: A Handbook for Middle Level Leaders, first published in 1996, provided many educators with assistance in instituting teaming. This new enlarged edition provides considerable additional information to help middle schools raise teaming to higher levels.

Chapter 1 provides the backdrop for the remainder of the book by sharing the rationale for teaming. The many benefits that accrue to both students and teachers, and to the curriculum and instruction practices are presented.

Reviewing the various arrangements of teams in a middle school is one component of Chapter 2. The other component challenges middle schools to consider new organizational arrangements that will include all teachers on teams, improve communication, and develop more opportunities for connections across the curriculum.

Scheduling is the theme of Chapter 3. Special attention is given to the numerous variables that affect scheduling in a middle school and to block scheduling which encourages creative approaches to making time support instructional goals.

Chapter 4, a completely new chapter, helps small middle schools develop the teaming concept. Facing unique problems because of size and such issues as teachers with multiple teaching assignments, this chapter offers a number of teaming models to generate creative solutions to team designs.

Chapter 5 explores some of the fundamental characteristics of effective teams. It challenges teams to establish measurable goals and to determine the extent to which they have been achieved. How to make team meetings more effective is clarified. The various stages of development that teams go through on their journey to high performance are explained. New sections on developing trust on teams and the importance of team members' nonverbal behaviors have been added.

The importance of the team leader and the need to clarify and strengthen this role on a team has emerged as perhaps the single greatest factor in the movement toward high performance teams. Along with identifying the critical responsibilities of the team leader, Chapter 6 includes a new section on decision-making styles for team leaders and the leadership function of this position.

The principal plays a key role in developing and nurturing teams. The principal's understanding and commitment to teaming will have a direct bearing on its effectiveness. With the leadership of the principal working in concert with team leaders, teams will have a greater opportunity to achieve their potential. These topics are shared in Chapter 7.

Staff development is mandatory if teaming is to produce intended results. Activities appropriate for staff development when implementing teaming are presented. To support the improvement of teaming, Chapter 8 has been expanded to assist those middle schools that are committed to raising their level of teaming. Of particular interest is a section on incorporating technology into instructional activities.

In the 1996 edition, decision making, problem solving, and conflict management were introduced. Because of the importance of these three major team skills, they are treated in separate chapters: decision making in Chapter 9, problem solving in Chapter 10, and conflict management in Chapter 11. The content in each chapter has been augmented with more examples to assist practitioners.

Chapter 12 focuses on a difficult topic, dysfunctional teams. Bringing a small group of professionals together to function as a team does not always result in harmonious relationships. Three levels of managing dysfunctional teams are explored.

A new concept is introduced in Chapter 13, the merging of the power of teaming with advisory programs. Suggestions are provided on how this merger can utilize the strength inherent in a teaming program to assist in the implementation and management of the difficult advisory program.

In order to improve the performance of teaming in middle schools, current practices must be continually assessed. Chapter 14 provides several ready-to-use instruments that can be administered by middle school personnel to assess the level of effectiveness of their teaming program.

Chapter 15 concludes the book by offering readers a variety of resources on the topic of teaming.

The middle school community has learned a great deal with the implementation of teaming over the past three decades. We have learned that teaming can have a very positive effect on students' attitudes and on achievement. We have learned that teachers in teams reach a higher level of professionalism and experience greater personal satisfaction. We have learned that the opportunities for connecting and integrating the curriculum are enhanced significantly with teams. We have learned these things largely through trial and error by dedicated personnel in middle schools. We have also learned that the ultimate goal of teaming – improved student learning – is not met without extensive effort to exploit the full potential of teaming. We must not stop and accept the status of teaming as it stands presently. We need to improve all aspects of teaming if we are to meet the demands of teaching and learning in middle level schools in the twenty-first century. ❑

1

Teaming in the Middle School

Companies in the 1990s are realizing that a diverse group of people – using their own creativity, innovation, judgment, intuition and brain power – can do a better job in today's world of constant change than any set of formal procedures, methods, or controls administered by a remote, centralized management.

– Thomas A. Kayser

Today's society, with change as the only constant, demands organizations that can embrace and respond to change. If middle schools are to meet the demands of the new millennium, organizational arrangements of schools must change just as they are changing in the business world. In middle schools, these changes will bring individuals together to work as teams and establish a climate of collegiality.

Peter Scholtes (1992), says: "... rarely does a single person have enough knowledge or experience to understand everything that goes on in a process. Therefore, major gains in quality and productivity most often result from teams — a group of people pooling their skills, talents, and knowledge." This statement, describing the synergism teams create, must become the *modus operandi* to improve teaching and learning in a middle school.

Teaching is itself an increasingly complex task. In an age when information is doubling every two years, teaching students how to retrieve, analyze, synthesize, and evaluate information must become a focal point of the curriculum. When technology is expanding at an astronomical rate, being able to incorporate technology into the instructional program is a significant challenge. When society has a growing number of one-parent families and families with both parents working outside the home, dealing with young adolescents and their unique needs is especially challenging.

Teachers are already overextended and cannot be expected to work longer and harder, but they can be placed on teams where they can work smarter. Putting teachers with complementary knowledge and skills on a team results in amassing talent that exceeds the capabilities of any single teacher. Teams of teachers can be more responsive to changing events and demands than an individual or an entire institution.

An interdisciplinary organization provides many advantages for students and teachers. It also improves communication and leads to improvements in communication, curriculum, and instruction.

Advantages for students

By bringing together several teachers and a common group of students, teaming creates a small caring family as suggested in *Turning Points — Preparing American Youth for the 21st Century* (Carnegie Council on Adolescent Development, 1989). Teachers come to know their students very well and students become comfortable with a small group of teachers. Interacting with a small group of students ensures that no student will go unnoticed. Teachers are more cognizant of changes in student behavior and can offer assistance when needed. Every child in this family environment will come to know at least one adult well. In time of need or personal trauma, it is important that students feel confident approaching an adult for assistance. These two possibilities – teachers knowing students and students knowing teachers – ensure a climate in which academic learning and personal growth can occur.

Advantages for teachers

When a team of two to five teachers is aligned with approximately 50-125 students, a consistent set of classroom management procedures can be established. Uniformity in the ways used to deal with such matters as being tardy, leaving the classroom, chewing gum, and covering books will benefit young adolescents who are already confused on a number of developmental issues. When several teachers decide collectively how to handle the problems of particular students and then work together to implement their plan, the potential is great for changing the behavior of these students. In like manner, consistency in routine instructional procedures such as late work, makeup work, and coordination of due dates will be valuable for both students and teachers. Ways of assessing and reporting student progress will be most effective when developed cooperatively by the team and communicated to students and parents.

A great sense of professionalism among teachers develops through teaming. Heretofore, teachers seldom met with one another to discuss professional issues. Now during common planning time, team members assist and support one another. Working to-gether to help a student overcome a difficult problem improves all teachers' competence. Providing assistance to others when needed generates confidence and self-esteem. Utilizing the strengths of one another creates synergy on the team.

Teaming provides opportunities for teacher involvement in decision making and leadership. It challenges teachers to take the lead in making decisions about curriculum and instruction that will benefit students. Teams involved in the hiring process and structuring the induction program for beginning teachers are engaged in a professional activity. Involvement in these two areas strengthens the relationship between teachers and administration.

When teachers work as a team, they come to understand students' behavior better, assist one another in growing professionally, and experience a much higher level of satisfaction and enjoyment with their work.

Advantages for communication

In a teaming structure, common planning time provides opportunities for teachers to communicate with and tap the expertise of counselors, special education teachers, media specialists, and the administration. Perhaps the greatest opportunity for improved communication is between team and special education personnel. Constant interaction between regular and special education teachers benefits all students on the team.

Communication with parents is significantly more effective when a team is involved. Discussing a particular student's situation within the team before contacting the parents is valuable. When parents can meet with several teachers at one time, benefits accrue to both parents and teachers. Progress reports are appreciated; by making this type of communication a team effort, the chance of parents' receiving regular proficiency reports is enhanced.

Advantages for the curriculum

Many, if not most, students view the curriculum as a set of disjointed and disconnected experiences. In a middle school with an interdisciplinary organization, teachers not only become aware of the content of various disciplines as a result of meeting with colleagues on a regular basis but they make connections. Teaming allows the coordination of teaching learning skills such as reading, problem solving, and information retrieval. Knowing the topics to be taught in other disciplines, teachers can sequence their curriculum to teach related topics at the same time. This leads to

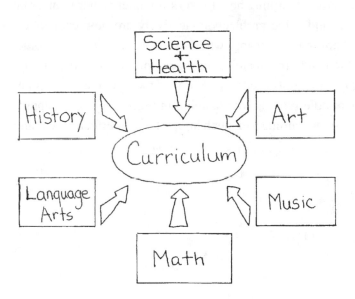

discovering opportunities that will move toward integrating the curriculum. Having teachers regularly discuss the curriculum can result in significant changes in the content and instruction provided students and is potentially the greatest benefit of teaming.

Advantages for instruction

All teachers possess certain instructional strengths. Teachers with special expertise in such areas as cooperative learning, technology, and assessment procedures can share information with others as well as model them. Occasionally, a teacher with a particular strength might team teach a lesson with another teacher or exchange classes to utilize this strength for the benefit of students. Beginning teachers particularly are served well when effective teaching strategies are shared and modeled.

Summary

Teaming allows people to work in new ways to stay abreast of the informational and technological society in which we live. It brings new demands for teachers and administrators. Learning how to work together rather than alone and to make decisions and solve problems collectively are new challenges. Teaming requires a commitment to change which will not come easily for some. Yet the possibilities created with a teaming arrangement are so numerous and desirable, *all* middle level schools need to give serious thought to its full implementation. For those middle schools with teaming in place, the time is appropriate to raise the quality of teaming to a much higher level of effectiveness and efficiency. ❏

2

Team Designs

The student should, upon entering middle grade school, join a small community in which people – students and adults – get to know each other well to create a climate for intellectual development.
— **Turning Points: Preparing American Youth
for the 21st Century**

Many factors affect the design of teams in a middle school. Because each middle school is different, it is important to understand various designs in order to create the most effective teams. This chapter focuses on team arrangements involving mathematics, science, social studies, and language arts plus several arrangements that include one or more encore courses. In addition, a number of designs that place all teachers on teams are described.

The term "core" used here, refers to mathematics, science, social studies, and language arts courses. All remaining courses in the middle school are termed "encore." This is an attempt to move away from designations such as academic/non academic, academic/related arts, and core/exploratory all of which imply, unfairly, a hierarchy.

CORE/ENCORE TEAM DESIGNS

Two-teacher team

The two-teacher team, Figure 1, is used increasingly in grade six as a sound transition from a single-teacher, self-contained classroom in the elementary school to the four- or five-teacher team commonly found in grades seven and eight. In this arrangement, one teacher may have primary responsibility for math and science, while the other is responsible for social studies and language arts, Each may also teach a section of reading. Courses taught can depend on the strengths and interests of each teacher. Both teachers would need multiple certification or a general elementary certification allowing them to teach all subjects. This model allows teachers and a group of students to spend a larger portion of the day together, strengthening the bond between them. Time can be used more flexibly, and more opportunities are available to make connections between the subjects.

Figure 1

Two-Teacher Team

50-60 Students	
TEACHER A	TEACHER B
Math	Social Studies
Math	Social Studies
Science	Language Arts
Science	Language Arts
Reading	Reading

Three-teacher team

The three-teacher team, Figure 2, is similar to the two-teacher team, except that all teachers have primary responsibility for one subject and a section of the two remaining subjects. Other ways of dividing the instructional responsibilities are also possible. It requires three teachers with multiple certification or general middle level certification. As with the two-teacher team, students stay with one team member for an extended period of time. This model provides for more flexible use of time and greater opportunities to connect the curriculum.

Four-teacher team

The four-teacher team, Figure 3, is the most commonly used and most logical composition with one teacher specialist in each of the four core areas. It allows teachers with a single subject certification to teach on the team. The four teachers may, of course, also engage in interdisciplinary planning and have an additional teaching responsibility beyond the core block to complete their workload. This model best utilizes teachers with strong content preparation in one subject area.

Figure 2

Three-Teacher Team

75-90 Students		
TEACHER A	TEACHER B	TEACHER C
Math	Science	Social Studies
Math	Science	Social Studies
Math	Science	Social Studies
Language Arts	Language Arts	Language Arts
Reading	Reading	Reading

Figure 3

Four-Teacher Team

100-120 Students			
TEACHER A	TEACHER B	TEACHER C	TEACHER D
Math	Science	Language Arts	Social Studies
Math	Science	Language Arts	Social Studies
Math	Science	Language Arts	Social Studies
Math	Science	Language Arts	Social Studies

Four-teacher team across two grade levels

This four-teacher arrangement, Figure 4, combines students across two grade levels. It is used when there is an insufficient number of students to complete a four-teacher single-grade team. While solving a numbers problem, it also creates the opportunity for a team of teachers to stay with a group of students for two years, a practice that has come to be called *looping*.

Figure 4

Four-Teacher Team Across Grade Levels

50 - 60 Seventh Grade Students 50 - 60 Eighth Grade Students			
TEACHER A	TEACHER B	TEACHER C	TEACHER D
Math 7	Science 7	Language Arts 8	Social Studies 8
Math 7	Science 7	Language Arts 8	Social Studies 8
Math 8	Science 8	Language Arts 7	Social Studies 7
Math 8	Science 8	Language Arts 7	Social Studies 7

Four-teacher team with a resource period

This design, Figure 5, requires core teachers to staff a resource period in addition to teaching four classes. All students and all teachers on the team are scheduled into this resource period. The resource period is extremely flexible because it allows teachers to regroup students for remediation, make-up testing, enrichment, or other activities. It is an excellent design to increase the opportunity to provide for the individual needs of students. Furthermore, it resolves the issue of a teacher assigned to four classes when the normal teaching load is five.

Four-teacher team with encore courses

In this model, Figure 6, the mathematics, science, social studies, and language arts teachers teach five sections of each subject. During each of the periods, four sections of students are enrolled in courses taught by team members while one group of twenty-five students leaves the team to take an encore course. This model allows a team of four teachers to teach five sections of students. The disadvantage is the limitation on the use of flexible scheduling.

Figure 5

Four-Teacher Team with a Resource Period

100-120 Students			
TEACHER A	TEACHER B	TEACHER C	TEACHER D
Math	Science	Language Arts	Social Studies
Math	Science	Language Arts	Social Studies
Math	Science	Language Arts	Social Studies
Math	Science	Language Arts	Social Studies
Resource Period	Resource Period	Resource Period	Resource Period

Figure 6

Four-Teacher Team with Encore Course

125-150 Students				
TEACHER A	TEACHER B	TEACHER C	TEACHER D	ENCORE TEACHERS
Math	Science	Language Arts	Social Studies	Encore Course
Math	Science	Language Arts	Social Studies	Encore Course
Math	Science	Language Arts	Social Studies	Encore Course
Math	Science	Language Arts	Social Studies	Encore Course
Math	Science	Language Arts	Social Studies	Encore Course

Five-teacher team

A teaming arrangement of five teachers with 125-150 students can be implemented if a fifth course such as reading is required for a full year of all students as depicted in Figure 7. While reading and language arts are shown as separate courses, they could be integrated into a communication course. Having reading as a course on the team can result in greater attention to reading in all remaining core classes.

Figure 7

Five-Teacher Team

125-150 Students				
TEACHER A	TEACHER B	TEACHER C	TEACHER D	TEACHER E
Math	Science	Language Arts	Social Studies	Reading
Math	Science	Language Arts	Social Studies	Reading
Math	Science	Language Arts	Social Studies	Reading
Math	Science	Language Arts	Social Studies	Reading
Math	Science	Language Arts	Social Studies	Reading

Five-teacher team with semester encore courses

In some middle schools, no fifth subject is required for an entire year. Under these circumstances, two required semester equivalent courses can be scheduled during the same period in a five-by-five arrangement. In Figure 8, music and physical education are offered on an alternate day basis. The music and physical education teachers are allied with two teams requiring them to meet for common planning on alternate days with both teams. It is an attempt to bring together as parts of one team both core and encore courses.

Five-teacher team with quarter encore courses

This arrangement is similar to the five-teacher team with semester courses shown in Figure 8. However, four courses, each nine weeks in length, are combined with the mathematics, science, social studies, and language courses to complete the matrix. Each of four encore courses is rotated through the team for nine weeks. For example, during the first quarter, all students on the team are enrolled in art, during the second quarter in technology education, in health during the third quarter, and in family and consumer education in the final quarter. The encore teachers work with four teams to complete the cycle. Figure 9 shows the example of art as the course aligned with the core courses.

Figure 8

Five-Teacher Team with Semester Encore Courses

125-150 Students				
TEACHER A	TEACHER B	TEACHER C	TEACHER D	TEACHER E/F
Math	Science	Language Arts	Social Studies	PE/Music
Math	Science	Language Arts	Social Studies	PE/Music
Math	Science	Language Arts	Social Studies	PE/Music
Math	Science	Language Arts	Social Studies	PE/Music
Math	Science	Language Arts	Social Studies	PE/Music

Figure 9

Five-Teacher Team with Quarter Encore Courses

125-150 Students				
TEACHER A	TEACHER B	TEACHER C	TEACHER D	ENCORE TEACHER
Math	Science	Language Arts	Social Studies	Art
Math	Science	Language Arts	Social Studies	Art
Math	Science	Language Arts	Social Studies	Art
Math	Science	Language Arts	Social Studies	Art
Math	Science	Language Arts	Social Studies	Art

MODELS PLACING ALL TEACHERS ON TEAMS

Interdisciplinary teams, in most middle schools, include language arts, mathematics, social studies, and science. While creating such teams has been a significant step forward, teachers not assigned to teams often feel disenfranchised. They, too, desire to work in small-group settings experiencing the collegial support that comes with teaming. In this section, several models are presented that place all teachers on teams. These attempt to accommodate the core/encore arrangement as described in the preceding section. Since no two middle schools are identical, there is a need for a variety of models to match these programs. Middle school personnel should examine these models and make the necessary adaptations or use the ideas presented to create a new model that fits their particular situation.

Overlapping core classes

Figure 10, shows three teams, one at each grade level, with the time of the day when students are scheduled in their core and encore courses. From 11:42 until 1:18, the core classes overlap. With all students in their core classes, the encore teachers can engage in team planning or individual preparation. This model could work in larger schools with two or three teams at one grade level.

This model requires the encore teachers to be available to teach students from each grade at designated times. Thus it places a premium on a required curriculum for all students. Further, this model is difficult to schedule when exploratory or specialist teachers in a middle school are shared with the high school, the elementary school, or with other middle schools. While requiring a cooperative scheduling agreement with other buildings, the results of placing encore teachers on a team are worth the effort.

Activity period schedule

An activity or enrichment period of approximately thirty minutes is included in the daily schedule in a number of middle schools. In the model illustrated in Figure 11, the activity period is scheduled at the end of the day. During this activity period, all students can be assigned to the core teachers on one or more days, providing meeting time for encore teachers. The amount of common planning time available is not equivalent to core teachers' planning time, but it does

Figure 10

Overlapping Core Courses

Sixth Grade Team

8:00		11:42	1:18	2:54

Core	Encore

Seventh Grade Team

8:00	9:36	11:42	1:18	2:54

Core	Encore	Core

Eighth Grade Team

8:00	9:36	11:42	1:18	2:54

Encore	Core

Figure 11

Activity Period Schedule

	Activity Period
Instructional Periods	Encore Planning Time

provide some meeting time for encore teachers within the school day. In a large school with numerous encore teachers, several encore teams should be developed.

Core/encore teams

In this model, it is assumed that core teachers have six classes, an individual preparation period, and a common planning period. Likewise, encore teachers teach six classes, have an individual preparation period, and are assigned to one of the core teams for planning. In most middle schools, the common planning time for core teams is spread across all periods of the day as shown in Figure 12. This model does place all encore teachers on teams; but since encore teachers often teach students from more than one grade level, encore teachers may find themselves aligned with a team where they share few students in common.

Figure 12

Core/Encore Teams

Period	Team Planning
1	Team 6A
2	Team 6B
3	Team 7A
4	No teams meet
5	Team 7B
6	Team 8A
7	Team 8B
8	No teams meet

SUMMARY

Teams should be designed to support the instructional program of the school. Initial efforts with team designs were almost exclusively restricted to various combinations of the basic academic or core areas. Several slight modifications have been developed to include encore subjects on the core teams, but they are relatively rare. The middle school community must not be satisfied with current designs but move ahead and create new ones that include all teachers on teams and thereby release the full potential of teaming.

Teaming in the middle school is a powerful organizational structure, and models of team designs must be sought that will take advantage of the potential of teaming. Evidence is beginning to mount indicating smaller teams of two-or three teachers have many advantages over larger teams of four or more teachers. Small teams allow teachers to know students better, increase the degree of individual attention teachers can provide students, and make team meetings more efficient, thus allowing teams to give greater emphasis to curriculum and instructional activities. ❏

3

Organizing and Scheduling Teams

*It is difficult to point to a single aspect of a middle school
that has as much impact on the children and adults as does
the schedule.* – Jeffrey S. Craig

Generating an initial schedule that accommodates teaming can be
difficult and time-consuming. Scheduling is dependent on numerous
factors which must be considered before the master schedule is developed. In this section, the placement of students and teachers on teams is
examined, the variables that affect scheduling are explored, the concept of a
master schedule is described, and examples of block scheduling are provided.

PLACEMENT OF TEACHERS AND STUDENTS ON TEAMS

Size of teams

Generally, the larger the team, the more difficult it is for it to function effectively. Teams of two to four teachers are most workable. Two-person teams are
especially appropriate for students coming from self-contained classrooms with
a single teacher. Two- and three-person teams most often need teachers with
multiple certification, while larger teams can utilize teachers with single or
dual certification. The important thing to recognize about teams with only two
or three teachers is the automatic reduction in the number of different students
taught and the accompanying increase in the amount of time a teacher and a
student are together. The reduction in the student-teacher ratio has many inherent and long-term advantages.

Of particular importance is the need to have all teachers on the team teach
all students on the team. Only if that premise is strictly adhered to will the
desired bonding occur between teacher and student. In some instances, eight
teachers and more than 200 students have been designated a team. This is a
misuse of the term particularly when many students have any combination of

teachers instructing them. This model violates the concept of a small group of teachers connecting with a small group of students in a family unit. Furthermore, team planning, a very valuable commodity, is extremely inefficient because not all teachers can enter into conversations about individual students since they may not have them in class, and the variety of personalities makes real collaboration difficult if not impossible. Where it is possible to schedule the teachers from two teams into a common planning time, the teams could meet occasionally as a large group to coordinate some grade level activities.

The number of encore teachers in a building will vary depending on enrollment, course offering, and shared teachers. When encore teams are formed, care must be taken to keep them small to be effective.

Placement of teachers on teams

Assigning teachers to teams is one of the principal's most important tasks. Chapter 7 describes various methods for placing teachers on teams and the principal's role in aligning teams. The basic goal, of course, is to develop teams that can work harmoniously and professionally. It is important to note that a team of diverse individuals who can function in a collegial manner will be stronger than a more homogeneous team. With diversity comes a greater range of background experiences and abilities to generate creative ideas for teamwork.

When placing teachers on teams, not only should the principal be concerned about harmony on the team but the special skills and interests that teachers bring to the team. Having one team with a group of teachers all with skills in technology while teachers on another team do not possess these attributes creates an uneven balance between teams that negatively affects students.

Length of tenure on teams

Because it often takes two or three years to become a smoothly functioning unit, changes in team membership should be made only for significant reasons. Unfortunately, in a closed situation, taking a person who is dysfunctional on one team and placing that individual on another team can disrupt the second team. Only after all efforts have been made to correct the problems of the dysfunctional team should a change in team membership be considered. This includes changing team membership where members may get along with one another very well but perform at a low level. Chapter 12 provides more detailed information on dysfunctional teams.

While the principal's evaluation of all teams' performances is ongoing, at the conclusion of each school year definite steps must be taken to help low-functioning teams improve. Sometimes this does mean making changes in team membership. If it is necessary to replace a team member, remaining team members should be asked to identify their skills and interests with the intention of locating a new team member who has skills and interests to complement the team and bring it to a higher level of performance.

Placement of students on teams

When placing students on teams, the overriding consideration is to create a quality learning opportunity for *all* students. Teams should be as close to "equal" as possible with no stigma attached to any team. Those forming teams should consider gender, achievement levels, special needs, and cultural differences. Placing a large number of students with special needs on one team and none on another, for example, creates an imbalance that has significant repercussions on the curriculum offered and the instructional procedures used.

In large schools with three teams at a single grade, it is permissible to place learning disabled students on one team, emotionally disabled students on another team, and cognitively disabled on the third team. By doing this, all teams have students with special needs, and it is easier to align teachers of special needs students with single teams.

Sectioning of students

Perhaps the best way to place students on a team into sections is to assign this task to the team members. Allowing them to section students often results in a better mix of individuals than if done by the principal or a computer. Team members should be allowed to move students from one section to another on their team whenever they believe the change is educationally beneficial. Moving students from one team to a different team is a much more serious decision and should be done only in special situations.

Criteria for sectioning of students should be discussed with all team members. If a school is attempting to reduce ability grouping, then this should be evident in decisions made by teams when they create the student sections.

Number and length of instructional periods

The time that school activities begin and end obviously determines the number of minutes available for instruction, lunch, and other activities. Middle school personnel usually have little to say about these matters since they hinge on bus schedules and other administrative factors. The total number of minutes available, the length of the lunch period, and the inclusion of an activity period are factors that impact the number of minutes assigned for instructional periods. The more time available for instruction, the greater the number of periods that can be created from this time or the longer times for each period. A study of Wisconsin middle schools, Figure 13, showed a decided preference for the eight period day so students can have more exploratory opportunities (Rottier, Landon, & Rush 1995). In other states the seven-period day is the norm.

Figure 13

Number of Instructional Periods

Number of periods	Percent of Schools Reporting
6	1
7	22
8	62
9	8
Other	6

Advisor-advisee/activity program

Many middle schools set aside 20-30 minutes each day for an advisory and/or student activity program. This block of time can be scheduled at various points during the day. Scheduling the advisory/activity period at the beginning or end of the day increases the number of contiguous instructional periods if block scheduling is desired for teams. Other schools provide an advisory period once, twice, or three times a week.

Nutrition breaks

The report, *Turning Points: Preparing American Youth for the 21st Century* (1989) published by the Carnegie Corporation's Council on Adolescent Development, reminds us of the importance of providing for the health and fitness of students in our middle schools. The business world provides workers with breaks to increase their efficiency. This should apply to students as well. Furthermore, in our current society, many students come to school without breakfast or with a breakfast of soda and potato chips. A nutritional break, especially in the morning can assist growing students whose bodies need nourishment. It also provides an opportunity for very legitimate student socialization, and some schools provide for such with no nutrition involved.

Two procedures are used most often to schedule the nutrition or social break. Providing an extended passing time between two classes allows students to mingle at certain places in the building. This procedure requires supervision in the gathering places. Another procedure is to lengthen one class period in mid-morning by approximately ten minutes. Each teacher provides students with break time in his/her classroom and is responsible for supervision. In middle schools with block scheduling, breaks can be scheduled by the team when appropriate with students remaining in the team area during the break.

Team meetings

The heart and soul of an interdisciplinary structure is common planning time for the team teachers. During this time, teachers discuss student, instructional, and curricular concerns. A major scheduling issue is the amount of meeting time necessary for a team. The most desirable arrangement is to schedule one period of common planning time each day *in addition to* an individual preparation period for each teacher. Where this is not possible, the minimum acceptable time for actual team planning is two periods each week; anything less severely limits the effectiveness of the team. A few middle schools, in their desire to implement teaming, have asked teachers to do their team planning before or after school. This is an invitation to disaster, because such time will slowly dissipate due to conflicts before and after school. It is unwise to ask teachers to substitute team planning time for their individual planning time. In this situation, individual planning will soon take precedence over team planning. If teams cannot be provided a minimum amount of common planning time during the school day in addition to individual planning time, they cannot be expected to do any real curriculum integration or otherwise exploit the potential of teaming.

Curriculum

The curriculum has a significant impact on the daily schedule. When teaming is implemented, several concerns appear.

- Coursework
  Schools often make curricular changes when they implement teaming. Middle schools need a strong mission statement and definite goals to provide guidance for making curricular decisions. If these goals do not exist, traditional practices, teacher preferences, and/or the concerns of vocal parents will direct the curricular changes.

- Tracking
  The greater the extent of tracking, the more difficult it is to schedule students. Establishing special classes for certain students reduces the unity so important when establishing teams and interferes with the flexibility provided by a block schedule. The extensive research on tracking ought to be thoroughly analyzed and evaluated. The less tracking, the better. If a middle level school is highly tracked, personnel may wish to implement a long-range (3-5 years) detracking goal to minimize the negative effects of tracking on students as well as on scheduling. Schedulers must be cognizant of de facto grouping, especially in smaller schools. Algebra, music, and foreign language may, for example, influence significantly the scheduling of classes for all students.

- Required versus elective courses
  Elective courses have a significant effect on scheduling. When students are allowed to elect courses, the task of those generating the schedule is to place the largest number of students in their top choices. When there is a prescribed curriculum for all students, establishing blocks of time for teams and team planning time is easier to achieve.

In some middle schools, the encore courses are taught by teachers shared with the elementary and/or high school. As result, the curriculum in the middle school is dependent on the availability of these shared teachers. Therefore the middle school curriculum changes from year to year. Middle school personnel need to decide on a curriculum that meets the needs of all students and work to make that curriculum available each year.

- Time allocation for each course
  The amount of time devoted to each course may constitute a major hurdle for schools implementing teaming. The perceived importance of a course is often equated with the amount of time assigned to it; for example, a semester course may be perceived to be twice as valuable as a quarter course. To fit all courses into a schedule that includes team planning time and block scheduling, it may be necessary to consider six-, nine-, twelve-, and eighteen-week courses along with full-year courses.

TEAM DEVELOPMENT AND SCHEDULING

Shared teachers, teacher certification, and teacher workload are items that affect the assignment of teachers to middle school teams and scheduling.

Shared teachers

In middle schools, especially those in small rural areas, sharing teachers with the high school or an elementary school makes the development of a master schedule with teaming very difficult. If a team of teachers shares a common group of students and has a common planning period, the team must be assigned to the middle school the same periods of the day. Block scheduling a team demands teacher presence in the building. When teachers must be shared, it is imperative to schedule these teachers into the middle school program first, although this may be contrary to existing practices.

A few middle schools, where encore teachers are shared with the high school, have done some creative scheduling so that a block of encore courses are taught to all middle school students at the same time during one period of the day.

This procedure allows core teachers to have common planning time while students are with their high school counterparts.

Some middle schools reduce the shared teacher dilemma by hiring teachers with multiple certification. This allows a team of two or three teachers to teach all the subjects, a situation with many advantages. (See Chapter 2 for a description of two- and three-person teams.)

Middle schools with extensive sharing of teachers must establish a long-term (3-5 years) goal to reduce or eliminate this practice to improve scheduling of teams. Once this plan is established, personnel and curricular decisions are approved only if the goal of reducing or eliminating shared teachers is advanced.

Teacher certification

When teams are being organized, the certification of teachers assigned to the middle school will need careful examination as teacher certification will play an important role in the team development. Where certification hinders team arrangements, schools must establish a plan to match teacher certification with team needs or seek a waiver from the state department.

Some teachers may need to extend their license to include all grades in the middle school or an additional subject field. When the Eau Claire, Wisconsin, school district placed grade six in the middle schools, teachers needing grade six added to their license submitted a portfolio of middle level staff development experiences. Working with the University of Wisconsin-Eau Claire, most were able to extend their license without taking additional coursework.

Teacher work schedule

The teacher workday requirement has a significant impact on the development and scheduling of teams. In a school with a seven-period day, the typical work requirement for a teacher is five classes, one supervisory responsibility, and one individual preparation period. Arrangements in schools with eight period days include five classes, one supervisory responsibility, and two individual preparation periods, or six classes, one supervisory responsibility, and one individual preparation period. Most middle schools have eliminated study halls, thereby reducing the need for that supervisory task. Substituting common planning time for this supervisory activity is a more professional use of teacher time. Teachers not on teams continue their supervisory responsibilities where needed.

The teachers' work schedule most often is negotiated with the school board. Therefore, changes to the existing contract must be discussed with the teacher organization and the school board.

DEVELOPING THE MASTER SCHEDULE

For teachers to have common planning time, their students must be involved in other classes during team planning. A master schedule indicating how this is accomplished is shown in Figure 14. For grade six, the students take their encore classes during periods one and two and their core classes during the remaining periods. Since the same teachers who teach the encore classes in grade six teach these courses to seventh and eighth graders, the encore classes for grade seven occur later during periods three and four and in grade eight during periods six and seven. This allows the core teachers in each grade to meet as a team when their students are in encore classes. If there is more than one core team in a grade, the schedule below could be adapted to use with one grade. Note that grade seven has a split core schedule. Rotating this split period of time over three years gives each team an opportunity for a continuous block of time.

Figure 14
Core Teacher Schedule

Period	1	2	3	4	5	6	7
6th Grade	Encore		Core				
7th Grade	Core		Encore		Core		
8th Grade	Core					Encore	

During the time that a core team's students are in the encore classes, the core teachers have their individual and team planning time as depicted in Figure 15. Note that during period five, all students are in the core classes allowing time for the encore teachers to meet as a team. (See Chapter 2 for a more detailed explanation of common planning time for encore teachers.)

Figure 15

Master Schedule

Period	1	2	3	4	5	6	7
6th Grade	Team	Prep	Core				
7th Grade	Core		Team	Prep		Core	
8th Grade	Core					Team	Prep

BLOCK SCHEDULING

Block scheduling provides a team of teachers contiguous instructional periods during the school day. Because students are not scheduled for courses other than those taught by team members, the team has complete control of the time allocated to them.

Use of this block of time is limited only by the creativity and initiative of the team. On opposite ends of the continuum on how the block is used are the assignment of equal periods of time for each discipline on the team and a field trip for the entire block of time wherein all students and all team members participate. Between these two extremes are innumerable possibilities for the team. The team can utilize the "pep-rally" schedule, often used in the high school, where a small amount of time is subtracted from each class period to create a period of time in which all students and all teachers are free of class. This time can be used to have team assemblies, videos, speakers, award programs, talent shows, or for giving a test to all students in one subject area. It offers tremendous opportunities to work with small groups of students on the team. For example, if several students did poorly on an exam, one teacher could meet with those students for reteaching while the remaining students are under the jurisdiction of the other teachers. Or, one teacher might offer interested students an opportunity to engage in a unique and challenging activity.

The seventh grade interdisciplinary team from Lyons Middle School in Clinton, Iowa, created numerous arrangements to make time fit the instructional needs of the team. Several of their schedules are depicted below.

Normal schedule

Figure 16 shows the normal schedule when teaming was implemented in Lyons Middle School. The students are involved in encore classes during the time preceding 10:20 A.M. while their teachers are either planning as a team or engaged in individual preparation. When students come to the area of the building to start their core block, a sign in the hallway indicates the location they are to go to at 10:20. At this point, they receive the schedule for the remainder of the day.

Figure 16

Normal Schedule

Time	Activity
8:00-10:20	Encore
10:20-11:05	Class
11:05-11:35	Lunch
11:35-12:20	Class
12:20-1:05	Class
1:05-1:25	Homeroom
1:25-2:10	Class
2:10-2:55	Class
2:55-3:17	Homeroom

Research and re-teaching

If all students are working on research projects, this schedule allows them to come together at one time either in the library or some other location to utilize the project materials. This arrangement is also useful for reteaching a topic to a particular group of students. For example, if fifteen students did not show sufficient mastery on a test in one of the team courses, then during the 10:20-11:20 period, Figure 17, those fifteen students meet with a team member for a reteaching session while all remaining students are involved in an enrichment or other appropriate activity under the jurisdiction of the other teachers on the team.

Figure 17

Research and Re-teaching Schedule

Time	Activity
8:00 - 10:20	Encore
10:20 - 11:20	Research/Reteaching
11:20 - 11:50	Lunch
11:50 - 12:30	Class
12:30 - 1:10	Class
1:10 - 1:50	Class
1:50 - 2:30	Class
2:30 - 3:17	Class

Computer resource schedule

Often, the computer facility is not available during the entire day for classes. The schedule in Figure 18 allows the team to interchange class periods so all students have the opportunity to use the computer resources.

Figure 18

Computer Schedule

Time	Activity
8:00-10:20	Encore
10:20-11:15	Class
11:15-11:45	Lunch
11:45-12:30	Class
12:30-1:15	Class (Computers)
1:15-2:00	Class
2:00-2:45	Class
2:45-3:17	Homeroom

Assembly/video/test schedule

On some occasions, it is desirable to bring all students together for an assembly, to present a video, or to have students take a test. The assembly/video/test schedule in Figure 19 allows time at the end of the day for these activities to take place. The special event could be scheduled any period within the block of time.

These examples are just a few of the many schedules that are possible when a team has control over the time for classes. The block schedule provides almost unlimited opportunities for the team to creatively match time to the goals of instruction.

Figure 19
Assembly/Video/Test Schedule

Time	Activity
8:00-10:20	Encore
10:20-11:15	Class
11:15-11:45	Lunch
11:45-12:30	Class
12:30-1:15	Class
1:15-2:00	Class
2:00-2:45	Class
2:45-3:17	Assembly/Film/Test

SUMMARY

Many new variables occur when middle schools implement teaming. Scheduling is an extremely important task because it places students, teachers, and the curriculum in contact with one another for the purpose of quality teaching and learning. Principals and teachers responsible for scheduling must approach the task in a very enlightened, thoughtful, and careful manner. Developing the master schedule is not just an administrative task. It should reflect a commitment to the middle school philosophy and goals. The greater the commitment, the more time and energy will be spent in this endeavor, and a more productive master schedule will be the result. ❏

4

Teaming in Small Middle Schools

When people are dedicated to meeting
the needs of boys and girls, they will
find innovative and creative ways to get
the job done.

— Michael Allen, Ronnie L. Sheppard, and Diane Bath

Generally, the larger the school, the easier it is to develop a schedule that includes teaming and block scheduling. Small middle schools, whether a separate unit or inextricably tied to a high school or an elementary school, offer special challenges when designing teams and creating a credible master schedule.

In many small school districts the middle school shares teachers and facilities with the elementary and/or high school. These two factors tend to strongly influence the master schedule of the middle school. Experience has shown that a middle school can operate effectively even though teachers and facilities are shared. However, to schedule a teaming arrangement requires careful planning and cooperation between units.

TEAM DESIGNS FOR SMALL SCHOOLS

The following team designs can be used in middle schools with small enrollments. A number of examples are provided depicting schools with seven or eight instructional periods.

To make it easy to interpret the tables that depict team designs, the courses to be taught by team members are assigned to periods one-five or one–six with individual planning time and team planning shown in periods seven and eight. While blocking the classes is the ideal arrangement, practical considerations such as shared teachers and shared facilities may not allow this to occur in the schedule of a small school. In all the examples provided, care must be taken to designate one period where teachers assigned to the same team can share a common planning time. This is in addition to providing an individual preparation period for each teacher each day. Without appropriate time to plan together, teams can never be successful.

While smallness is typically viewed as a handicap, it also is a major plus in many middle school ways. As will be noted in many of the following examples, teachers teach the same pupils in more that one grade level, much in the manner of looping that has become a desirable trend. In like manner, two- or three-person teams, a necessity in small schools, are in line with the growing advocacy of partner or small teams.

Twenty-thirty students per grade
- Example one (seven-period day)
  Figure 20, depicting a three-person team, is shown in a seven-period day. Each team member is primarily responsible for one discipline at all three grade levels as well as teaching language arts and reading to a particular grade. If reading is not taught as a full-year course in grades seven and eight, teachers B and C might offer these students some special interest courses not available from encore teachers.

- Example two (eight-period day)
  In the example shown in Figure 21, two teachers are responsible for the four core courses for students in grades six, seven, and eight. Reading would be taught as an encore course to students in some or all three grades.

Figure 20

Three-Person Team/Seven Period

Period	TEACHER A	TEACHER B	TEACHER C
1	Math Grade 6	Science Grade 6	Social Studies Grade 6
2	Math Grade 7	Science Grade 7	Social Studies Grade 7
3	Math Grade 8	Science Grade 8	Social Studies Grade 8
4	Language Arts Grade 6	Language Arts Grade 7	Language Arts Grade 8
5	Reading Grade 6	Reading Grade 7	Reading Grade 8
6	Individual Planning	Individual Planning	Individual Planning
7	Team Planning	Team Planning	Team Planning

Figure 21

Two -Person Team/Eight Period

Period	TEACHER A	TEACHER B
1	Math Grade 6	Science Grade 6
2	Math Grade 7	Science Grade 7
3	Math Grade 8	Science Grade 8
4	Language Arts Grade 6	Social Studies Grade 6
5	Language Arts Grade 7	Social Studies Grade 7
6	Language Arts Grade 8	Social Studies Grade 8
7	Individual Planning	Individual Planning
8	Team Planning	Team Planning

Fifty-sixty students per grade
- Example one (seven-period day)

    Two teachers teach the core subjects of mathematics, science, social studies and language arts at each grade level along with a required full-year course in reading as shown in Figure 22. In a seven-period school day with teachers required to teach five classes, this constitutes a full teaching load for six teachers, assuming the remaining two periods are taken up by an individual preparation and a common planning time for each teacher. In this model, no teachers are shared and all teachers must have multiple certification. The six teachers are formed into three teams, two at each grade level

Figure 22

Six Teachers/Three Teams/Seven Periods

	Grade Six		Grade Seven		Grade Eight	
Period	TEACHER A	TEACHER B	TEACHER A	TEACHER B	TEACHER A	TEACHER B
1	Math	Social Studies	Math	Social Studies	Math	Social Studies
2	Math	Social Studies	Math	Social Studies	Math	Social Studies
3	Science	Language Arts	Science	Language Arts	Science	Language Arts
4	Science	Language Arts	Science	Language Arts	Science	Language Arts
5	Reading	Reading	Reading	Reading	Reading	Reading
6	Individual Planning Time	Individual Planning Time	Individual Planning Time	Individual Planning Time	Individual Planning Time	Individual Planning Time
7	Team Planning Time	Team Planning Time	Team Planning Time	Team Planning Time	Team Planning Time	Team Planning Time

- Example two (seven-period day)

In Figure 23, a seven-period day is depicted with no core teacher involved in teaching reading. This arrangement requires multiple teaching assignments by five teachers with one teacher in need of an additional assignment (Teacher E). Because the teachers have teaching assignments across grade levels, it is imperative that all five teachers have the same period for team planning. Individual teaching assignments are based on the qualifications and interests of the five teachers.

Figure 23

Five Teachers/One Team/Seven Periods

Period	TEACHER A	TEACHER B	TEACHER C	TEACHER D	TEACHER E
1	Math Grade 6	Language Arts Grade 6	Math Grade 7	Social Studies Grade 6	Math Grade 8
2	Math Grade 6	Language Arts Grade 6	Math Grade 7	Social Studies Grade 6	Language Arts Grade 8
3	Science Grade 6	Language Arts Grade 7	Science Grade 8	Social Studies Grade 7	Social Studies Grade 8
4	Science Grade 6	Language Arts Grade 7	Science Grade 8	Social Studies Grade 7	Social Studies Grade 8
5	Math Grade 8	Language Arts Grade 8	Science Grade 7	Science Grade 7	High School or Supervisory
6	Individual Planning	Individual Planning	Individual Planning	Individual Planning	Individual Planning
7	Team Planning	Team Planning	Team Planning	Team Planning	Team Planning

• Example three (seven-period day)

Many middle schools require a full-year course in reading for sixth grade students. In this example, shown in Figure 24, the sixth grade team of two teachers teach the four core areas and reading. The four teachers in grades seven and eight require an extra assignment to complete their teaching load. They could be assigned one course in the high school or a supervisory responsibility. If reading were taught as a semester course in grade seven and/or grade eight, one or more of the four core teachers in grades seven and eight could be assigned that responsibility.

Figure 24

Six Teachers/Three Teams/Seven Periods

	GRADE SIX		GRADE SEVEN		GRADE EIGHT	
Period	TEACHER A	TEACHER B	TEACHER A	TEACHER B	TEACHER A	TEACHER B
1	Math	Social Studies	Math	Social Studies	Math	Social Studies
2	Math	Social Studies	Math	Social Studies	Math	Social Studies
3	Science	Language Arts	Science	Language Arts	Science	Language Arts
4	Science	Language Arts	Science	Language Arts	Science	Language Arts
5	Reading	Reading	High School / Supervisory	High School / Supervisory	High School / Supervisory	High School / Supervisory
6	Individual Planning	Individual Planning	Individual Planning	Individual Planning	Individual Planning	Individual Planning
7	Team Planning	Team Planning	Team Planning	Team Planning	Team Planning	Team Planning

• Example four (eight period day)

In Figure 25, the teaching assignments of six teachers are shown for an eight-period day. To complete their teaching load of six classes, each teacher would need to be assigned a course to teach at the high school and/or some supervisory responsiblity. This example also requires multiple certification for all teachers.

Figure 25

Six Teachers/Three Teams/Eight Periods

Period	Grade Six		Grade Seven		Grade Eight	
	TEACHER A	TEACHER B	TEACHER A	TEACHER B	TEACHER A	TEACHER B
1	Math	Social Studies	Math	Social Studies	Math	Social Studies
2	Math	Social Studies	Math	Social Studies	Math	Social Studies
3	Science	Language Arts	Science	Language Arts	Science	Language Arts
4	Science	Language Arts	Science	Language Arts	Science	Language Arts
5	Reading	Reading	Reading	Reading	Reading	Reading
6	Individual Planning	Individual Planning	Individual Planning	Individual Planning	Individual Planning	Individual Planning
7	Team Planning	Team Planning	Team Planning	Team Planning	Team Planning	Team Planning
8	Supervisory Activity or Teach a Course at the High School					

- Example five (eight-period day)

  Four teachers teach the core subjects of mathematics, science, social studies, and language arts at three grade levels. In this model shown in Figure 26, each of the four teachers would teach two sections of seventh grade. Teachers A and B, forming one team could have separate team planning time from the team of teachers C and D, or a common planning time could be established for all four teachers if it is possible to schedule.

- Example six (eight-period day)

  In this example, each team member teaches one discipline to all students in grades six, seven, and eight as shown in Figure 27. This model allows the utilization of teachers certified in only one discipline. Reading, if required of some students, would be treated as an encore course taught by a teacher not necessarily aligned with the team of four teachers. It does require all four teachers to be available one period for common planning time.

Figure 26

Four Teachers/One or Two Teams/Eight Periods

Period	TEACHER A	TEACHER B	TEACHER C	TEACHER D
1	Math Grade 6	Language Arts Grade 6	Math Grade 8	Language Arts Grade 8
2	Math Grade 6	Language Arts Grade 6	Math Grade 8	Language Arts Grade 8
3	Science Grade 6	Social Studies Grade 6	Science Grade 8	Social Studies Grade 8
4	Science Grade 6	Social Studies Grade 6	Science Grade 8	Social Studies Grade 8
5	Math Grade 7	Language Arts Grade 7	Science Grade 7	Social Studies Grade 7
6	Math Grade 7	Language Arts Grade 7	Science Grade 7	Social Studies Grade 7
7	Individual Planning	Individual Planning	Individual Planning	Individual Planning
8	Team Planning	Team Planning	Team Planning	Team Planning

Figure 27

Four Teachers/One Team/Eight Periods

Period	TEACHER A	TEACHER B	TEACHER C	TEACHER D
1	Math Grade 6	Language Arts Grade 6	Science Grade 6	Social Studies Grade 6
2	Math Grade 6	Language Arts Grade 6	Science Grade 6	Social Studies Grade 6
3	Math Grade 7	Language Arts Grade 7	Science Grade 7	Social Studies Grade 7
4	Math Grade 7	Language Arts Grade 7	Science Grade 7	Social Studies Grade 7
5	Math Grade 8	Language Arts Grade 8	Science Grade 8	Social Studies Grade 8
6	Math Grade 8	Language Arts Grade 8	Science Grade 8	Social Studies Grade 8
7	Individual Planning	Individual Planning	Individual Planning	Individual Planning
8	Team Planning	Team Planning	Team Planning	Team Planning

Seventy-five to ninety students per grade

A number of options are available for scheduling a teaming arrangement with this number of students.

- Example one (seven-period day)

  This model is similar to the two-person team with 50-60 students. Three teachers, with multiple certification, would teach three sections of one discipline and each teacher one or two additional disciplines. See Figure 28. A team of three teachers is required for each grade.

Figure 28

Nine Teachers/Three Teams/Seven Periods

Period	GRADE SIX			GRADE SEVEN			GRADE EIGHT		
	TEACHER A	TEACHER B	TEACHER C	TEACHER A	TEACHER B	TEACHER C	TEACHER A	TEACHER B	TEACHER C
1	Math	Science	Social Studies	Math	Science	Social Studies	Math	Science	Social Studies
2	Math	Science	Social Studies	Math	Science	Social Studies	Math	Science	Social Studies
3	Math	Science	Social Studies	Math	Science	Social Studies	Math	Science	Social Studies
4	Language Arts	Language Arts	Language Arts	Language Arts	Language Arts	Language Arts	Language Arts	Language Arts	Language Arts
5	Reading	Reading	Reading	Reading	Reading	Reading	Reading	Reading	Reading
6	Individual Planning	Individual Planning	Individual Planning	Individual Planning	Individual Planning	Individual Planning	Individual Planning	Individual Planning	Individual Planning
7	Team Planning	Team Planning	Team Planning	Team Planning	Team Planning	Team Planning	Team Planning	Team Planning	Team Planning

- Example two (seven-period day)

  A number of schools do not offer a reading course in grades seven and eight. Figure 29 indicates a team of three teachers in grade six and a five-person team covering grade seven and eight. One teacher would need an additional assignment for one period.

Figure 29

Seven Teachers/Two Teams/Seven Periods

Period	Teacher A	Teacher B	Teacher C	Teacher D	Teacher E	Teacher F	Teacher G	Teacher H
1	Math Grade 6	Science Grade 6	Social Studies Grade 6	Math Grade 7	Science Grade 7	Science Grade 8	Social Studies Grade 8	Language Arts Grade 7
2	Math Grade 6	Science Grade 6	Social Studies Grade 6	Math Grade 7	Science Grade 7	Science Grade 8	Social Studies Grade 8	Language Arts Grade 8
3	Math Grade 6	Science Grade 6	Social Studies Grade 6	Math Grade 7	Science Grade 7	Social Studies Grade 7	Social Studies Grade 8	Language Arts Grade 8
4	Language Arts Grade 6	Language Arts Grade 6	Language Arts Grade 6	Math Grade 8	Science Grade 8	Social Studies Grade 7	Language Arts Grade 7	Language Arts Grade 8
5	Reading Grade 6	Reading Grade 6	Reading Grade 6	Math Grade 8	Math Grade 8	Social Studies Grade 7	Language Arts Grade 7	High School
6	Individual Planning	Individual Planning	Individual Planning	Individual Planning	Individual Planning	Individual Planning	Individual Planning	Individual Planning
7	Team Planning	Team Planning	Team Planning	Team Planning	Team Planning	Team Planning	Team Planning	Team Planning

- Example three (seven-period day)

  Figure 30 depicts a program where reading is offered in grades seven and eight with this assignment taught primarily by one teacher. This creates a team of three teachers for grade six and a large team of six teachers for grades seven and eight.

- Example four (eight-period day)

  In this example shown in Figure 31, three teams of two teachers are created to teach this number of students. However, these team members are not responsible for teaching reading.

Figure 30
Nine Teachers/Two Teams/Seven Periods

Period	Teacher A	Teacher B	Teacher C	Teacher D	Teacher E	Teacher F	Teacher G	Teacher H	Teacher I
1	Math Grade 6	Science Grade 6	Social Studies Grade 6	Math Grade 7	Science Grade 7	Science Grade 8	Social Studies Grade 8	Language Arts Grade 7	Reading Grade 7
2	Math Grade 6	Science Grade 6	Social Studies Grade 6	Math Grade 7	Science Grade 7	Science Grade 8	Social Studies Grade 8	Language Arts Grade 8	Reading Grade 7
3	Math Grade 6	Science Grade 6	Social Studies Grade 6	Math Grade 7	Science Grade 7	Social Studies Grade 7	Social Studies Grade 8	Language Arts Grade 8	Reading Grade 7
4	Language Arts Grade 6	Language Arts Grade 6	Language Arts Grade 6	Math Grade 8	Science Grade 8	Social Studies Grade 7	Language Arts Grade 7	Language Arts Grade 8	Reading Grade 8
5	Reading Grade 6	Reading Grade 6	Reading Grade 6	Math Grade 8	Math Grade 8	Social Studies Grade 7	Language Arts Grade 7	Reading Grade 8	Reading Grade 8
6	Individual Planning	Individual Planning	Individual Planning	Individual Planning	Individual Planning	Individual Planning	Individual Planning	Individual Planning	Individual Planning
7	Team Planning	Team Planning	Team Planning	Team Planning	Team Planning	Team Planning	Team Planning	Team Planning	Team Planning

Figure 31
Six Teachers/Three Teams/Eight Periods

Period	Teacher A	Teacher B	Teacher C	Teacher D	Teacher E	Teacher F
1	Math Grade 6	Social Studies Grade 6	Math Grade 7	Social Studies Grade 7	Math Grade 8	Social Studies Grade 8
2	Math Grade 6	Social Studies Grade 6	Math Grade 7	Social Studies Grade 7	Math Grade 8	Social Studies Grade 8
3	Math Grade 6	Social Studies Grade 6	Math Grade 7	Social Studies Grade 7	Math Grade 8	Social Studies Grade 8
4	Science Grade 6	Language Arts Grade 6	Science Grade 7	Language Arts Grade 7	Science Grade 8	Language Arts Grade 8
5	Science Grade 6	Language Arts Grade 6	Science Grade 7	Language Arts Grade 7	Science Grade 8	Language Arts Grade 8
6	Science Grade 6	Language Arts Grade 6	Science Grade 7	Language Arts Grade 7	Science Grade 8	Language Arts Grade 8
7	Individual Planning	Individual Planning	Individual Planning	Individual Planning	Individual Planning	Individual Planning
8	Team Planning	Team Planning	Team Planning	Team Planning	Team Planning	Team Planning

- Example five (eight-period day)
  This example, shown in Figure 32, includes a full-year reading course for sixth grade students along with a semester course of reading for grades seven and eight. The reading teacher would need to meet with both teams during team planning time.

Figure 32

Six Teachers/Three Teams/Eight Periods

Period	Teacher A	Teacher B	Teacher C	Teacher C	Teacher D	Teacher E	Teacher F
1	Math Grade 6	Social Studies Grade 6	Reading Grade 6	Math Grade 7	Social Studies Grade 7	Math Grade 8	Social Studies Grade 8
2	Math Grade 6	Social Studies Grade 6	Reading Grade 6	Math Grade 7	Social Studies Grade 7	Math Grade 8	Social Studies Grade 8
3	Math Grade 6	Social Studies Grade 6	Reading Grade 6	Math Grade 7	Social Studies Grade 7	Math Grade 8	Social Studies Grade 8
4	Science Grade 6	Language Arts Grade 6	Reading Grade 7/8	Science Grade 7	Language Arts Grade 7	Science Grade 8	Language Arts Grade 8
5	Science Grade 6	Language Arts Grade 6	Reading Grade 7/8	Science Grade 7	Language Arts Grade 7	Science Grade 8	Language Arts Grade 8
6	Science Grade 6	Language Arts Grade 6	Reading Grade 7/8	Science Grade 7	Language Arts Grade 7	Science Grade 8	Language Arts Grade 8
7	Individual Planning	Individual Planning	Reading Grade 7/8	Individual Planning	Individual Planning	Individual Planning	Individual Planning
8	Team Planning	Team Planning	Team Planning	Team Planning	Team Planning	Team Planning	Team Planning

ENCORE TEAMS IN SMALL MIDDLE SCHOOLS

Small middle schools with shared teachers seldom can create an encore team with teaching responsibilities involving only middle school students. Small schools have been successful in working collaboratively with high schools and elementary schools so all core teachers can have a common planning time while students are enrolled in encore classes.

SMALL MIDDLE SCHOOLS AND HIGH SCHOOL BLOCK SCHEDULING

Some small middle schools are linked to a high school that utilizes a block schedule where students take a limited number of classes each day with the class periods being 80–90 minutes in length. This type of schedule is not incompatible with teaming at the middle level, because one extended period at the high school can be equivalent to two periods at the middle school. Thus teachers can be shared without too much difficulty. For example, a team of four teachers with 100 students in the middle school requires four periods of teaching for each of four teachers on the team enabling each of the teachers to teach one 80-90 minute course each semester in the high school which completes their full teaching load. The key to making this arrangement work is cooperation between the middle school and the high school.

SUMMARY

Teaming is such a powerful organizational strategy that it should not be limited to medium and large middle schools. Sharing teachers and facilities with elementary and high schools makes scheduling in a middle school difficult. It may be necessary to create some combinations of teams, even if less than desirable, in order to get started. It should be recognized that the smallness itself is a major plus. Perhaps the program of teaming needs to be phased in over a period of time. Most often, it is necessary to create a long-term plan to reduce the impediments to an effective teaming arrangement. When that is the case, all curricular and personnel changes must be made only when they enhance this desired goal. ❏

5

Characteristics of Effective Teams

The essence of synergy is to value the differences, to respect them, to build on strengths. – Stephen Covey

Teacher preparation programs in the past have focused on helping each person become the best possible teacher in the classroom. Few efforts were made to encourage or prepare prospective teachers to work with one another. Effective teams do not result, however, from placing several people trained to work independently on a team and then charging them with a set of expectations that require collaboration.

This chapter focuses on the characteristics of effective teams including setting team goals, defining roles of team members, and establishing basic ground rules for effective team meetings. Because the behavior of team members has a significant effect on team productivity, the following topics are addressed: interpersonal behaviors, nonverbal behaviors, developing trust, participation-discussion rules, and team celebrations. The stages that groups go through on their way to becoming high performance teams are also discussed.

TEAM GOALS

The most effective teams have clear goals and a commitment to work toward those goals. Each year, near the close of the spring semester, interdisciplinary teams should assess their current goals and establish new ones for the following year. Goals will likely involve curriculum, instruction, and assessment; they may focus on the social and emotional behaviors of students, improving communication, developing a positive climate, and/or connecting with parents.

Typical team goals

Following are some typical goals for interdisciplinary teams.

- Design and teach a designated number of thematic units, some based on student interests and concerns
- Plan social activities and field trips for students
- Make greater use of the flexibility available with the block schedule
- Meet with all the parents of students on the team
- Improve the communication with encore teachers
- Continue the development of a positive climate
- Make greater use of technology in the instructional program
- Involve encore teachers in team activities
- Involve the team in a service learning project

An examination of these goals indicates they are written for the teachers, and that it is difficult to determine if a team has successfully met such general goals.

New goals

While the goals above are all desirable ones, teams will increase their effectiveness by refocusing the emphasis away from what the teachers do and move toward identifying the direct impact on students. Goals should be challenging, explicit, and measurable, thereby providing specific direction to the team. Furthermore, the team must identify criteria by which it can determine if its objectives have been met. Below is a list of goals that focus on students and provide explicit direction for teams. Writing the goals with "…at least _____ percent" encourages the team to go beyond the stated criterion.

- Increase the average daily attendance of students by at least _____ percent
- Increase parent attendance at conferences by at least _____ percent
- Increase the participation of students in clubs and activities by at least _____ percent

- Decrease missing assignments by at least _____ percent
- Decrease discipline referrals to the office by at least _____ percent
- Decrease incidents of disruptive behavior outside the team by at least _____ percent
- Increase parent involvement in school activities by at least _____ percent
- Decrease gender imbalance in student activities by at least _____ percent
- Increase student involvement in team social activities by at least _____ percent
- Increase student achievement on the state mathematics test by at least _____ percent
- Increase student achievement on the persuasive writing portion of the state English test by least _____ percent
- Increase student opportunities to connect with adults in the building by at least _____ percent
- Increase the number of students who begin class having eaten a healthy breakfast by at least _____ percent
- Increase student attendance at school events, involvement in the science fair, color day, etc. by at least _____ percent
- Increase the number of students who use peer mediation by at least _____ percent
- Decrease drug and alcohol referrals by at least _____ percent
- Decrease tardiness to school by at least _____ percent

Teams are encouraged to consider establishing goals using these as examples to stimulate their thinking. Of particular value is an analysis of the results of statewide testing. In Wisconsin, schools are provided with an item analysis allowing the staff to identify specific weaknesses. This information could be most valuable when teams are goal setting. Other states have testing programs that provide specific data useful in setting team goals.

Selecting and assessing goals

Teams must give careful consideration to the selection of goals and decide how they can meet them. Once selected, the team should examine curriculum, teaching strategies, climate, and all other facets of their program that impact the goals. Plans to implement, monitor, and assess the goals must be established at the time they are chosen. Chapter 10 provides some tools for collecting and analyzing data.

Selecting measurable goals carries with it the risk of failure. However, not reaching an established goal can be valuable. When analyzing the data collected on a goal, it is important to determine why the goal was not reached and what might be done to achieve it in the future.

The task of collecting and portraying data for the assessment of a goal could be done by the mathematics teacher with the help of students on the team. The mathematics teacher could obtain the data and use them in a learning activity with students. Results in the form of student-generated charts and graphs might be displayed in the team area to inform and motivate students. Many of the goals stated above could be handled in a similar fashion involving students in the data collection and reporting of the results. Furthermore, some goals lend themselves to classroom discussions that will lead to improved student performance.

TEAM ROLES

Possible team roles are described in Figure 33. Having each teacher on the team assume one or more of the team responsibilities is an excellent means of building team unity and interdependence. Indeed, dividing the workload is the only way all team responsibilities can be accomplished.

The three roles of *leader, recorder,* and *liaison* are essential. Other roles with concomitant expectations including ones not mentioned here can be established at the discretion of the team. It is important that role assignments not be done on a seniority basis or any other system that prevents all members from full participation on the team. To create a sense of belonging on a team, each team member should be responsible for at least one ongoing responsibility.

In addition to the roles described above, teams may find it valuable to have each team member serve as a resource person related to a particular issue or project. A good example is technology. Technology is developing at such a rate that no one person can stay on top of the new programs available to middle level teachers. If a team decides to integrate technology into its curriculum

Figure 33

Team Roles

Role	Responsibility
Leader	Provides leadership. (See Chapter 6 for a detailed explanation of the team leader role.)
Recorder	Keeps a record of actions and decisions made by the team and serves as the team historian.
Team Liaison	Communicates with the administration, other teams, encore teachers, support staff, and others to obtain or share information.
Gatekeeper	Provides feedback to members of the team, especially when there are dysfunctional behaviors evident. (Examples include dominating, withdrawing, and antagonizing behaviors.) May also serve as timekeeper.
Resource Person	Obtains and manages resources needed to implement team activities. Serves in a consultative capacity to other members of the team.
Public Relations	Keeps people informed about the many activities and accomplishments of the students and faculty on the team; prepares news stories.
Social Activities	Organizes social activities for students and teachers on the team.

whenever possible, it makes sense to develop technology resource persons on the team. Each team member could select one area of technology in which sh/e would be the "expert" and serve as the resource person for other team members and students on the team. Some areas of technology that might be developed include presentation software, database files, the Internet, software that creates charts and graphs, and desktop publishing programs. Not only would a team member provide assistance to other team members, but when it becomes necessary to teach students how to use this technology, teachers might exchange classes or team teach the topic to students.

Team records

The maintenance of complete team records is imperative. These records make it possible to trace team activities and decisions. Of specific importance are records of discussions and actions on behalf of students. These records will be important when conferring with parents or recommending major changes in a student's program. In addition, an accurate record of team activities will be invaluable if critics of teaming seek to reduce or eliminate common planning time.

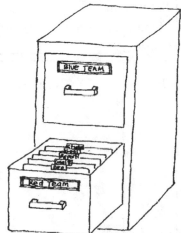

Recordkeeping can be simplified by using a form such as the one portrayed in Figure 34. A standard form will help to ensure the recording of pertinent information on all team activities over a period of time.

GROUND RULES

Every team must establish rules to govern its operation. Known as ground rules, they help each member display the behaviors necessary to make teaming function smoothly. A number of suggested ground rules follow.

Meeting time

Common planning time takes place within the confines of a regularly scheduled period. Since a majority of schools have class periods in the 40-50 minute range, it is important to maximize the use of limited time. Teams must establish a precise starting and ending time. For example, if the period begins at 10:03, the team could establish 10:06 as the time to begin the meeting. If the class period ends at 10:45, the team might declare 10:42 as the ending time in order to enable them to return to their classrooms for the next class. In this example, there are 36 minutes of meeting time. If

Figure 34

Recordkeeping Form

Team Name:		Date: _____	
Members Present:			
Guests: _____			

Item	Team Action	Person Responsible	Target Date

one person is five minutes late, the meeting time is reduced by 14 percent. An effective team cannot conduct business without all members present for the entire meeting. It would be well for a team to determine the personnel cost to the school district for one team planning period and then ascertain if the school district is receiving an honest return for its investment.

Attendance

Attendance at team meetings is as mandatory as being in class to conduct teaching responsibilities. Other than an emergency, the only reason to be absent from a team meeting is being legally absent from school. Skipping meetings to do other work must be treated as a very serious breach of contract. The principal must establish this requirement when teaming is first introduced and occasionally remind all faculty of this requirement. The principal supports this mandate by not scheduling activities that interfere with team meetings. District-wide activities such as curriculum writing should be scheduled to minimize the number of times team members will be absent. Lack of attendance or tardiness to team meetings is an obvious symptom of a dysfunctional team.

Meeting place

The team meeting location should be consistent so team members do not question its whereabouts each day. The best meeting place is one devoted solely to team meetings where external stimuli are not present as they may be when meetings are held in a classroom. The room should be equipped with a large table, comfortable chairs, one or more filing cabinets, a writing board, a bulletin board, and possibly a telephone.

Having a place devoted solely or primarily to team planning sets a positive climate for meetings. It sends a strong message about the importance of common planning time. New middle schools should include a team workroom/office/meeting area located in an appropriate location.

Interruptions

When teams are planning, personnel in the building all too often interrupt them to communicate with one or more team members. Team members may unconsciously be encouraging these interruptions by allowing people to come into the meeting with no advance warning. Teams must establish the importance of the meetings and convey this message to others in the building. The team might place the following sign on the door: "Team Meeting in Progress: Please Do Not Disturb." Initially this may be viewed as rude, but personnel in the school will soon respect the desire to conduct effective team meetings. Anyone desiring to speak to the team during team planning time should contact the team leader and be placed on the agenda of an upcoming meeting or catch members before or after the formal meeting. School receptionists should be aware of team meeting schedules and take messages for any team member receiving a call during team planning time. It may be helpful if the team recorder makes a note of each interruption in the team's

minutes. Reviewing this information may help the team become more aware of the intrusiveness of interruptions and the source of them.

TEAM MEMBER BEHAVIORS

The behavior of team members plays a significant role in the productivity level of a team. Where team members are cognizant of their behaviors and their effects on others, teams have a better chance of working together toward common goals. Some of those behaviors are discussed in the following section.

Interpersonal behaviors

A survey of teachers about the interpersonal behaviors and characteristics necessary for members of effective teams resulted in this list:

student centered	trustworthy
respectful	honest
team player	sense of humor
listener	professional
cooperative	patient
consistent	positive
committed to the team	supportive

During staff development prior to teaming (see Chapter 8), these characteristics should be discussed. When determining team goals, members could select one or more of these interpersonal behaviors to pursue. The team should discuss ways of helping members acquire and display these characteristics and conduct an assessment each quarter to determine progress on these goals.

Nonverbal behavior

High performing teams communicate effectively. Often the importance of nonverbal behaviors is given limited consideration. Yet nonverbal behaviors on teams will either have a positive effect on team communication or be a significant impediment to effective communication.

Below is a list of positive and negative nonverbal behaviors identified by middle level teachers. Not only should team members be aware of these behaviors, but the team leader should be constantly assessing these behaviors and how they are affecting team communication.

- **Positive nonverbal behaviors**

nodding	eye contact	smiling
leaning forward	taking notes	thumbs up gesture
actively listening	touching	being attentive

- **Negative-non-verbal behaviors**

rolling eyes	fidgeting	yawning
doodling	shaking of head	reading
grading papers	frowning	daydreaming
finger tapping	leaving	staring
no eye contact	leaning backward	packing up materials to leave

Participation/discussion rules

To ensure full participation of everyone in the meetings, team members should agree on a number of basic procedures. Below are some rules that might be adopted by a team.

- Everyone contributes equally.
- Each person must indicate her/his true feelings before decisions are made.
- Members speak freely on any topic without criticism.
- All listen attentively, courteously, and openly to ideas expressed.
- Everyone can express a viewpoint without being interrupted.
- Members stay focused on the topic under discussion.
- Members will refrain from side conversations.
- Members will not correct papers or engage in other personal activities

Ground rules should be established and reviewed each year. When team composition changes, rules must be reexamined. Once in place, ground rules should be posted in the team meeting room as a reminder of team expectations.

TRUST

Of all interpersonal behaviors on teams, perhaps none is more important than trust. Trust not only affects how we react to other team members as persons but as professional colleagues. When we trust someone, we have a reasonable chance of predicting his/her behavior. When teams are first formed, team members do not exhibit a high level of trust since they have not interacted with one another and are not able to predict how individuals will react and respond to team issues. Trust develops over a period of time when behaviors become reasonably consistent.

Team members can help develop the attribute of trust in ways such as the following.

- Keep commitments. When a team member makes a promise to the team and follows through on the commitment, trust moves to a higher level.
- Respect others. Whether we agree or disagree with someone, respecting the right to an opinion should not result in put-downs or any other behaviors that send deprecating messages.
- Maintain open communication. When a person limits or stops communicating, confusion results which places the trust level in danger of decreasing.
- Supporting others. By supporting others, we communicate our belief in the value of their opinions and improve the trust level.

When the level of trust is high, team members are willing to take risks and feel comfortable about the ensuing behaviors of their teammates. This allows the team to seek new and creative ideas to deal with issues facing the team.

Team leaders are responsible for monitoring the trust level of the team. If signs indicate the trust level is decreasing, the team should take time to review the situation in order to maintain the high quality of teaming. Teams need to realize that trust is not built in a short period of time; however it can be destroyed very quickly and needs to be worked on continuously.

TEAM CELEBRATIONS

Celebration is rejoicing when something positive has been accomplished or an individual's achievements are recognized. Celebrating achievement increases the possibility of continued or greater performance on the part of the individual. In a similar way, noting the achievements of teams may move them to higher levels of performance. Likewise, recognizing and rewarding students on the team will help to ensure a repetition of the behavior that was the basis of the recognition.

Team celebrations should not be an end-of-year activity; celebrations are appropriate whenever a team has accomplished a goal, reached a major decision, solved a thorny problem, or resolved a conflict. Students on the team can be rewarded for notable achievements, good behavior, and/or for progress made in a particular area.

Chapter 15 contains two lists of celebration ideas identified by middle school teams. Teams using the lists need to determine what kind of celebration is congruent and appropriate to the accomplishments or behavior of students or teams.

STAGES OF TEAM DEVELOPMENT

All successful teams, whether in professional sports, business, or education, go through a series of predictable stages from the initial gathering of group members to reaching a high performance level. Intertwined in these stages are distinct feelings and behaviors of the individuals relative to the concept of teaming. Many authors discuss stages of team development with special recognition given to the pioneering work of Bruce W. Tuckman (1965).

Stage One

In this initial stage, a group of individuals comes together in the quest to function as a team. While most individuals have positive feelings about the group's potential to achieve certain tasks, some may be ambivalent or even hostile to the team concept. Group members may have a general idea where their journey will take them but often are confused about how the group can achieve its goals.

Many teams find it very comfortable to remain a Stage One team. Planning time activities focus primarily on student concerns, housekeeping duties, and communication items. None of these require the team members to make uncomfortable and difficult decisions. Teams may make some attempts to move to a higher stage but find they come to areas of discomfort such as curricular

and instructional decisions. Lacking the skills of decision making, problem solving, and conflict management, teams find it easiest to stay at the Stage One level.

Stage Two

Stage Two is sometimes characterized as the political or power stage. Some members of the team will exert considerable influence on the team while others withdraw. Personal agendas may abound. Ground rules will be tested. Often the morale of the team is quite low. This happens when a group of people realize the efforts and sacrifices necessary to function as a team while not possessing the skills needed to accomplish these tasks. Depending on the ex-

tent of the arguing, bickering, and other types of negative behaviors, the productivity level may not increase very significantly.

When teams realize they have entered this stage, it is imperative they receive staff development training in decision making, problem solving, and conflict management. If not, the team will not progress to a higher level and may very well regress to the comfort of Stage One.

Stage Three

If individuals on the team are able to recognize problems they are having, if there is a belief that by working together the team can overcome these problems, and if the team has the skills of making good decisions, solving problems, and managing conflicts, the team will move to a higher stage. Team members begin to recognize the strengths that each team member brings to the team and capitalize on these strengths. They become more comfortable working within the established ground rules and start to enjoy one another's presence. Often, they  share personal situations. They provide support for one another. Teams in Stage Three have greater skill in making decisions, solving problems, and managing conflicts resulting in greater productivity, satisfaction, and pride for team members.

Stage Four

This is the goal of any team – to reach a high level of productivity and personal satisfaction with teaming. A team in Stage Four finds it relatively easy to make decisions, solve problems, and manage conflicts. Members adhere to ground rules. They become reflective about the progress of the team and seek ways to keep the team performing at a high level. In a sense, all members of the team exert leadership, with the team leader playing the role of facilitator and coordinator.

It is difficult for a team to function continuously at this level; occasionally, it will drop back to Stage Three, but the nature of the team members is such that they will strive to regain their high performance level.

The speed at which a group of people can move from the gathering stage to one of high performance will depend on a number

of variables. The desire to function as a high performance team greatly influences movement through these stages. The skill of the team leader in providing direction and assistance will enhance the journey. A quality staff development program that develops a knowledge base and skills of teaming can ensure a proper start and continued success with teaming.

SUMMARY

When teams are formed, they face *task* issues and *people* issues. Task issues include setting goals, establishing roles, and developing decision-making, problem-solving, and conflict-management procedures. Setting ground rules such as meeting times, attendance, and discussion/participation rules to govern team behaviors comprise the people issues. In addition, attention must be given to the interpersonal behaviors of team members. Being aware of the significance of nonverbal behaviors and the development of trust among team members will help teams immensely in their pursuit of team effectiveness. Learning to celebrate team and student achievements will improve the team's performance.

Teams learn that high performance develops in stages. Being aware of these stages will help teams progress with a minimum of frustration.

It is no longer acceptable to permit teams to remain at Stage One focusing almost exclusively on student behavior, housekeeping chores, and communication items. While these are worthwhile team planning time activities, teams must move forward with a much greater emphasis on curricular and instructional issues that affect student achievement. Only then can middle schools begin to justify the costs inherent in teaming. ❏

6

The Team Leader

*A successful leader has to be innovative. If
you're not one step ahead of the crowd you'll
soon be a step behind everyone else.*

— Coach Tom Landry

Too little attention has been paid to the role of the team leader in an
interdisciplinary organization. In fact it has come to be recognized as
a major weakness in the development of effective teams. The role of
department chair has been long established with its primary focus on carrying
out routine duties including ordering supplies and materials and assisting with
the development of the department budget. Seldom were department chairpersons expected to provide real leadership in student development, curriculum
development, or instructional improvement that is the professional development of their colleagues.

In many middle schools the role of the team leader is poorly defined. To
assure that no one would get "stuck" doing whatever the team leader was supposed to do, often the role has been rotated among members each year or semester. However, it is increasingly clear that leadership is critical to the development of effective teams.

In a study of middle schools by George and Shewey (1994), 81 percent of
the respondents indicated that team leaders play an important role and have
contributed to the long-term effectiveness of the middle school program.

This chapter shares some characteristics of effective leaders, elaborates on
the numerous roles that team leaders play, the procedures used to select team
leaders and placement on teams, length of appointment and remuneration, and
the professional growth of team leaders. Decision-making styles for team leaders are identified and explained. Finally, suggestions are provided for team
leader behaviors that match the developmental stages of teams.

ROLE OF THE TEAM LEADER

Team leaders must fulfill a variety of roles that include six major responsibilities described on the following pages.

Selection of new team members

Traditionally, the principal made all decisions involved in the hiring of teachers. This was logical because each teacher reported directly to the principal. In a school with a teaming arrangement, however, it is the team leader who is in constant contact with staff members on the team. To ensure a harmonious relationship on the team and with the administration, the team leader ought to play a key role in selecting new players on the team.

The team leader, and often the entire team, should be involved in early discussions about replacing a team member and in writing the job description. Perusing credentials of applicants to select those persons who will be invited for interviews should be done in cooperation with the principal. All team members should be involved in the interview process. The formal selection of the person to be hired is done by the principal, but having the team leader involved

in all facets of hiring strengthens the importance of the team within the middle school.

Providing assistance to new team members

Team leaders must be constantly concerned with the professional development of team members. Teaming provides a superb induction program for teachers new to the school, especially if the new teacher is just making the transition from college to the classroom. In a nurturing environment, neophytes can gain a sense of pride and confidence in their role as a member of a team.

The team leader must work with all members of the team to help them perform at the top of their ability. While new teachers are quite willing and pleased to be assisted by the team leader, more experienced teachers may not be as willing. Thus the team leader needs to possess the leadership skills to interact successfully with all team personnel.

Developing curriculum

Teaming offers a small group of teachers enormous opportunities to shape the curriculum for the benefit of their students. Meeting on a daily basis provides team members with ample opportunities to learn about one another's curriculum and how to collaborate. Team leaders play a key role in focusing discussion on improving the curriculum for students. If the team leader is committed to the concept of curriculum integration, this enthusiasm will be recognized by team members and can go a long way toward assisting in this endeavor. The team leader must recognize opportunities for integration and be willing to bring this opportunity to the attention of team members.

Managing student behavior

Teaming presents ample opportunities for achieving consistency among teachers in the management of student behavior. Helping team members develop common requirements in conjunction with their students and then encouraging consistency in applying these procedures is an important function of the team leader. Team discussions on behavior initiated by the team leader will help beginning teachers and those weak in classroom management skills gain confidence in this area.

Meeting the social needs of students

Team leaders need to ensure that an appropriate amount of team planning time is devoted to ways of meeting the social and emotional needs of students as well as their academic needs. Discussion of the particular needs of students can result in various ways of meeting them, including groupwork, class parties, socials, and field trips.

Managing resources

This role is similar to that held by department chairpersons. Team leaders assist teams in acquiring the resources necessary to meet instructional responsibilities and managing those resources in a prudent manner.

Communicating

A major role of the team leader is establishing good communication within the team and between the team and other constituencies in the school, including the principal, faculty, other teams, guidance counselors, nurse, parents, and the students themselves. This is done orally through a team liaison person and in written form through letters, notes, team meeting minutes, and team publications.

A TEAM LEADER'S JOB DESCRIPTION

It is extremely important to identify the expectations of team leaders in the middle school. Providing this information to prospective team leaders gives them the opportunity to determine if they really not only desire to apply for the team leader position but if they feel ready to accept this new professional responsibility. Having a clear set of expectations for team leaders provides a basis of support as they go about their duties. Making these expectations known to team members can clarify any misinterpretations of the responsibilities of the team leader relative to the team.

The principal should assume leadership in developing the team leader job description. Involving the staff in preparing this document will help ensure the acceptance of this person's role on the team. Using the team leader checklist provided in Chapter 14 will serve as an excellent starting point for generating a team leader's job description.

DESIGNATING TEAM LEADERS

Team members may become team leaders through rotation, selection by team members, or by administrative appointment.

Rotation

This procedure is used when no one person desires to be the team leader and the role is ill-defined. Rotational team leadership is based on the assumption that the team leader is expected to assume a variety of responsibilities that no one wants to do on a continuing basis; therefore, it is passed around among team members. This plan is obviously flawed in many ways. First, the team leader should not be expected to play all the roles involved in a team – leader, recorder, liaison, etc. Every member of the team needs to assume one or more roles. Second, not every teacher possesses the skills or the desire to be a team leader. Many teachers are excellent team members but experience frustration when asked to lead the team. Third, the role of the team leader is far too important to be handled in a happenstance manner. A key to the effectiveness of every team is how well the team leader exercises leadership in assisting the team in fulfilling its responsibilities. Rotational service does not bode well for the development of effective teams.

Selection by team members

While seeming like a very democratic procedure, selection by vote of the team members has the potential to be ineffective. Sometimes such a selection is based on popularity, experience, or because a particular person has an ax to grind and other team members feel they should or should not allow this individual to be the leader. Furthermore, there may be no one person on the team that desires to be a team leader or is willing to accept this responsibility. If we believe that team leaders can have a significant influence on the actions of the

team, this method of selecting a
team leader may not place the best
person in this important role.

Appointment by the principal

Having the team leaders appointed by the principal is the most
logical and appropriate method of
making this decision. The principal may invite potential candidates
for a team leader position to discuss the possibility and/or to apply. If the principal believes that
certain individuals have great potential to be team leaders, these

people should be encouraged to apply. Once those willing and able have been
determined, the principal can proceed with interviews and make assignments
that will have the greatest positive effect on the various teams.

It is important for the principal to match the qualities of the team leader with
the particular nature of the team. If a team is just beginning to work with the
concept of teaming, a team leader that can provide direction is especially important. If a team has been having difficulties, then a person who can play a
strong supportive role would be the best choice. In all cases, the principal must
accept the selection and placement of team leaders as an extremely important
responsibility.

TENURE, REMUNERATION, AND GROWTH OF TEAM LEADERS

Tenure

While each situation is distinctive, as a general rule, it is best for a team
leader to be appointed for a period of three years. The first year will be a professional growth experience. To reassign after one year means that year's experience is lost. It is also advisable to have an ending date for the assignment of
team leaders. First, it gives the team leader an opportunity to make a gracious
exit from the position after providing a term of service. Second, if the team

leader is doing only a mediocre job, it allows the principal to make a change rather easily. Third, this procedure opens the way for other teachers to prepare for and accept the challenge of being a team leader.

The principal should formally evaluate each team leader annually. These assessments should be viewed as an opportunity for team leaders to reflect on their effectiveness and, with the help of the principal, to grow in their abilities as team leaders. Certainly, a change in team leadership can and should be made earlier than three years when circumstances warrant a change.

Remuneration

The remuneration of team leaders, if any, will depend on many factors. Precedent, union contracts, and local budgets are among factors that determine how team leaders are rewarded. If the job description for a team leader requires work outside the school day, then in most middle schools this qualifies the person occupying this position for some remuneration. If it does not require outside activities, then perhaps no remuneration is required. Remuneration can be in the form of a stipend, released time, or extra perks. Released time from a supervision duty may be seen by some team leaders as more valuable than a stipend. Providing team leaders with financial support to attend conferences and workshops is an excellent way to reward these individuals for their efforts. Or, some combination of stipend, released time, and perks can be arranged. At any rate, the position of team leader is enhanced if some identifiable benefit is attached to it.

Professional growth of team leaders

All too few opportunities have been provided for team leaders to grow professionally by attending workshops geared specifically to improve their knowledge and skills. Some team leader training may be available from technical colleges that offer training for personnel in the business world. If this type of staff development is not available, the principal should facilitate some in-house staff development for team leaders. Since the effectiveness of a team hinges on the capabilities of the team leader, it is important that the principal arranges

staff development opportunities for team leaders through local activities, conferences, or at the least through professional reading.

LEADERSHIP FROM THE TEAM LEADER

Teams go through several stages on their journey to becoming high performing teams. At the different stages in team development, team members may act and feel differently about their tasks at hand and about one another. The journey to high performance is a continuous one and not marked by distinct lines of demarcation between the stages. Within each stage of development, the actions of team members change slowly as the team gains experience in the art of working together for the benefit of students.

It is important that the team leader be sensitive to the particular behaviors of team members in order to actively provide the appropriate leadership. In the sections below, the manner in which the leadership style of the team leader can be in concert with the stages of team development is described.

Leadership Scenario

To demonstrate appropriate team leader behaviors, the following
scenario presents actions the team leader must take for each stage
of team development. In the scene, Judy is the team leader; Manuel
is a first year teacher; Amanda is an experienced teacher but new
to the building, while Deb and Thomas are experienced teachers.
The team decided to take its students on a field trip some distance
from the school. The team leader needs to ascertain the stage of
development of the team and then plan how she will assist the team
in planning for the field trip.

Stage One

A team in the beginning stage might be a brand new group just making an
initial attempt at teaming or perhaps a group that has been together for some
time but one that has not progressed beyond Stage One. In this stage, team
members tend to be highly dependent on the personal wisdom and direction of
the team leader.

Therefore, the team leader should act in a fairly decisive and direct manner
by providing considerable structure to team activities. The team leader needs to
keep the vision of a quality team in mind when dealing with team members.
Helping the team set goals, assisting it with sorting out the different responsibilities of the team and who will perform each role, and establishing ground
rules and operating procedures are important leadership activities of the leader
in this stage.

If the team has just been formed, it is important that the leader help members
get to know one another. The team leader also needs to learn who are the assertive people, the risk takers, student centered, and who are really committed to
teaming. Knowing the strengths and concerns of each team member is imperative for the team leader when structuring team activities.

Getting everyone involved in team activities early in the team's development is a responsibility of the team leader. Communicating with individual
members and encouraging them to interact with one another helps to build
relationships that will serve the team well in the future.

Often, teachers who have been appointed to the leadership role are very concerned about how assertive they should be when providing direction to team members. They realize that when the team meeting is completed, they must function as a colleague of each of the team members. Good team leaders realize that a team in Stage One is seeking guidance and will react positively to a team leader who shows confidence and appropriate assertiveness.

Leadership Scenario (continued)

This is the first day of planning for the field trip, and Judy, the team leader, has judged her team to be in Stage One. Two major activities need to take place during the initial planning period – defining the tasks that need to be completed for an effective field trip and aligning each person on the team with a specific responsibility. Since a team in Stage One is seeking direction and will accept it from the team leader, an appropriate procedure would be to have Judy present a list of the major tasks to be completed to assure a successful field trip. She would assign Manuel and Amanda, teachers new to the district, their responsibilities and then ask Deb and Thomas, the experienced teachers, to take on other tasks for this field trip. Because this is the team's first field trip, Manuel and Amanda should be given the least complicated tasks, while Deb and Thomas, because of their experience, along with Judy would take on the more difficult tasks. Some team leaders begin by opening the floor to identify field trip responsibilities and allow members to volunteer to take on identified tasks. However, this is more appropriate for a higher functioning team.

Judy should indicate to her team members that in the future, when the team has had more experience functioning as a team, other procedures will be used to identify the tasks and align team members with responsibilities.

Stage Two

Discussing student behaviors, taking care of general housekeeping duties, and involvement in communication of day-to-day activities are worthwhile team endeavors. Most of these items do not involve major differences of opinion resulting in relatively easy decision making. However, some team members may want the team to move ahead with efforts in such areas as curriculum integration or investigating alternative assessment. These items require decision-making, problem-solving, and conflict management skills. When team members do not possess these skills, arguing, defensiveness, and blaming may occur which lead to a difficult time for team members.

Effective team leaders recognize when their team has become complacent and stagnant, unable to move beyond Stage One. Team leaders, with skills in decision-making, problem-solving, and conflict management should begin with the least contentious issues and attempt to apply consensus decision-making procedures to issues that all team members can agree on and support. Being able to utilize a few problem-solving tools will help team members address some sticky issues confronting them. Furthermore, being able to deal with differences of opinion in a systematic and objective manner will help the team move to higher levels of performance. When team members are exhibiting behaviors typical of Stage Two development, the team leader must redouble efforts to keep communication lines open in order to continue the positive team activities gained during Stage One. Reminding team members that it is in their best interest to work together is imperative.

Leadership Scenario (continued)

Judy has determined that her team is in Stage Two due to constant bickering about any issue that requires change from the status quo. While the team has agreed on the development of the field trip, she is aware that unless she handles the situation in a delicate manner, the field trip may fall apart and students will suffer because of it. Therefore she comes to the first planning meeting well prepared.

Knowing that in this stage brainstorming the tasks that need to be accomplished may not bring about the desired results, she provides the team with a list of the major responsibilities for a field trip and then asks if there are any additions to the list. With that task completed, she asks Manuel and Amanda to take on those responsibilities that do not require previous experience in the school district. She explains this to all four members and then indicates that she, Deb, and Thomas will pick up the remaining tasks.

By bringing in list of tasks to be accomplished, she avoids the possibility of a long and loose period of discussion that might lead to frustration and backing out of the field trip. She is a model of competence as she shares these tasks with the group. As for the assignment of tasks to individuals, she has avoided the possibility of the two teachers with experience in the district selecting those tasks which are the easiest thus requiring Manuel and Amanda to work on the most difficult tasks. These two tasks should be moved through with expediency to get team members so involved that backing out of the field trip is no longer viewed as desirable.

Stage Three

As teams develop their teaming skills and become comfortable with one another, team planning time will become both more enjoyable and productive. Team members, with greater respect for the differences and values each member brings to the team, will address issues of curriculum, instruction, and technology. The boredom that comes from continually harping on student problems during planning time will begin to disappear as teams search for productive activities that will benefit all students. Such teams reap the benefits of operating at stage three development.

The team leader continues to play an important role at this stage of team development. Most any issue or problem can be addressed without team members becoming upset and angry with one another as they now have strategies to deal with problems facing the team and some experience in using them.

It is important that the team leader keep a finger on the team's pulse. When dealing with significant issues, it is easy to fall back into the previous mode of arguing and bickering. Keeping the lines of communication open and flowing in both directions will prove beneficial to the team leader.

Leadership Scenario (continued)

A team in Stage Three, as Judy has now judged her team to be, should be able to make decisions without any significant difficulty. Therefore she decides to include the team in defining the tasks to be completed along with the assignment of roles to each person on the team. A brainstorming session is held, the tasks defined, and each person is asked to select a role to play in conducting an effective field trip.

Stage Four

Stage Four is the pinnacle of team productivity and performance. Skilled in decision-making, problem-solving, and conflict management skills, teams can tackle any issue with ease and are constantly on the lookout for new strategies to improve student learning. Being able to reflect on their progress, this is the team willing to take risks to improve the students' performance level.

Stage Four teams continue to require the support of the team leader. Because members may want to be on the cutting edge of educational reform, it is important that the team leader recognize the energy level required of teachers and help them avoid becoming so involved that mundane team activities are neglected.

Of significance at this level is the leadership that each team member can provide. True delegation exists where the team leader can request a member take over the responsibility of leading the team on a particular project.

Leadership Scenario (continued)

Each of the team members is able to assume a leadership role when a team is judged to be in Stage Four. With that in mind, Judy asks Thomas if he would be willing to assume the leadership role for planning the field trip. In addition, she sets a date when the team will discuss plans for the field trip and requests Thomas to come prepared to lead the project activity.

It should be recognized that seldom would a team reach Stage Four or even Stage Three during the first year of its existence.

SUMMARY

Although teams have become an integral component of middle schools, the role of the team leader has been undervalued. If middle schools are expecting teaming to reach its potential for improving student achievement, the best place to start is with the team leader position. The position is unique because the person in the role of team leader is a full-time faculty member and a colleague of the remaining members of the team. This uniqueness should not deter middle schools from strengthening this position through appropriate selection, assignment, and professional growth of team leaders. ❑

7

The Principal's Role in Teaming

Enlightened leaders know how to get their people
excited about their mission.

– Ed Oakley and Doug Krug

The principal plays a pivotal role in the development and implementation of teaming. Teaming calls for a fundamental change in the organizational structure. Instead of teachers reporting directly to the principal, in a teaming structure the principal interacts with teams as entities and with individual teachers primarily through the team leader. The change in structure brings concomitant changes in the role of the principal.

Principals must have a thorough understanding of and a belief in the interdisciplinary organization. The attitudes and actions of the principal can enhance or hinder the operation of teams both in schools where teaming is being initiated and in those schools with a history of teaming.

This chapter covers selecting and placing teachers on teams, monitoring and assisting teams, working with team leaders, and solving team problems.

SELECTING AND PLACING TEACHERS ON TEAMS

Assigning teachers to teams is a critical responsibility of the principal. Effective teams consist of teachers who are able to work harmoniously and creatively for the benefit of their students. Special care must be taken to ensure this harmony when the principal makes team assignments.

There are two basic ways to organize teams: have the principal assign teachers to teams, or have the principal collaborate with team leaders in making the placements. When the first strategy is used, the principal runs the risk of having insufficient knowledge of individuals who can work together in a collegial manner. Team leaders are generally in a better position to know the nuances of individual teachers. It may be valuable to ask each teacher, in a confidential manner, if there are any teachers with whom he or she would have difficulty working. This information can provide additional insights for the principal and team leaders as teachers are assigned to teams. If team leaders are appointed before teachers are assigned to teams, the collaboration of principal and team leaders is the preferred means of placing teachers on teams.

Except in very special circumstances, teachers should not select their team-mates. This procedure has the potential to create some super teams and other very poor ones. Furthermore, if a few teachers are not well liked by the major-ity of teachers, this self-selection process can exacerbate the situation.

When hiring new teachers, it is important to select people who will fit the team to which they are assigned The credentials of candidates should be exam-ined carefully to help determine if they have the potential to be team players. Perhaps a candidate was a member of a successful team in another school, or belonged to an athletic or forensics team at a university, or during student teach-ing had been placed with a teacher on a team. Experiences like these generally indicate that a person is likely to mesh with the team to which the individual is assigned.

A recommended procedure for filling a vacancy on a team is to ask the re-maining team members to fill out a job description for the new hire. Team members should identify the desired strengths of the new person that would complement the strengths of remaining team members. For example, if none of the existing members of the team have a great interest in technology, the job description for the new person should contain this characteristic. Other skills to complement a team include a special interest in interdisciplinary instruction, alternative forms of assessment, cooperative learning strategies or service learn-ing. The goal is to bring to a higher level the competencies of the team.

Team members should be involved in interviewing each candidate for the opening on their team. This is a great opportunity to involve teachers in crucial decision making. Furthermore, it places a stamp of importance on the concept of teaming in the school.

ALIGNING TEAM LEADERS AND TEAMS

When aligning team leaders and teams, the reactions of team members to the proposed team leader must be considered along with the potential of the person to lead the team. A team composed of inexperienced team members will benefit from a leader capable of providing direction and supervision. An experienced team that is functioning at a high level is better served by a leader capable of support and delegation. An appropriate match between team leader and team is crucial to the team's effectiveness.

MONITORING TEAM PERFORMANCE

The responsibilities of the principal continue after teams and team leaders have been selected. To ensure proper functioning, the principal needs to continue monitoring the progress of teams. There are several procedures that a principal can use.

The principal can manage by *wandering around*, to borrow a phrase popular in the business world. This implies that the principal leave the office and become aware of all that is happening in the building simply by being present in class-

rooms, team meetings, and hallways. Talking to students can determine their perceptions of how things are going on the team, and observing murals and hallway decorations will provide evidence of team activities. By visiting team meetings with some regularity, the principal can determine how effectively they are being conducted; however, principals must be aware that their presence at team meetings can change the nature of the meetings. Requiring team leaders to submit a weekly report on the activities of the team is an appropriate means of monitoring progress. Returning these reports with comments will strengthen the communication between principal and teams. Finally, meeting regularly with the team leaders builds a communication network between and among administration and teams and provides a support group for team leaders.

NURTURING TEAMS

While the team leader is responsible for providing direction to the team at each stage of development, the principal must provide team leaders with the assistance and support they need to carry out their responsibilities. The principal should provide overt commendations to those teams that are achieving their goals and working harmoniously through notes to teams, positive oral statements in staff meetings, and comments about team efforts in communications that go to parents.

Besides providing positive feedback to teams that are functioning well, the principal also has the more difficult and important task of nurturing teams having difficulties. It is important, of course, that the principal allow team leaders and teams an opportunity to resolve their own problems before becoming involved. The principal provides direction and support to the team leaders as they work through problems their teams are encountering before making any direct intervention in team affairs.

Too often the principal is caught up in a myriad of administrative duties and fails to pay attention to the effectiveness of teams until significant problems begin to appear. It is in the best interest of the principal to pay very close attention to team operations to ensure appropriate team behaviors. Unlike dealing with a single teacher who is having difficulties, working with a team of teachers who are not functioning well is a more formidable task. Unfortunately, there are instances where team members will band together to make life difficult for the principal. Rather than waiting for small problems to grow into larger problems, it is important that the principal pay strict attention to the progress of teams.

SUMMARY

Several benefits accrue to principals as a result of organizing the faculty into teams. The research of George and Shewey (1994) and others reveals that under teaming, discipline problems are reduced and teachers' sense of efficacy increases with no loss in achievement on traditional test reports. These changes assist the principal in fulfilling more of a leadership role rather than one of a manager. Newer responsibilities come with teaming. They include understanding the philosophy of teaming and how effective teams function, recognizing early warning signs of dysfunctional teams, and taking appropriate steps when a team is having difficulties. Principals must engage in personal professional staff development to accomplish effectively the tasks before them.

A principal assessment instrument relating to teaming in a middle school is provided in Chapter 14. ❏

8

Staff Development for Teaming

*The single distinguishing characteristic of the best
professionals in any field is that they consistently
strive for better results and are always learning to be
more effective, from whatever source they can find.*
                                    – Michael Fullan and Andy Hargreaves

Too many middle schools implement teaming with little or no preparation. Without appropriate staff development dealing with this powerful organizational strategy, teachers, team leaders, and principals are likely to become frustrated and students will realize few benefits from teaming.

This chapter presents staff development ideas for middle schools considering teaming as well as for schools already using teaming. For schools just adopting teaming, a number of staff development steps are described: understanding teaming, visiting quality middle schools, developing team leaders, building the team, establishing consistent expectations for students on teams, and ideas for team meetings. Follow-up staff development activities for schools with teaming include refocusing on team goals, clarifying roles, reaffirming ground rules, integrating the curriculum; and incorporating technology into the curriculum. Finally, restructuring team planning time is addressed and a suggested weekly schedule presented.

INITIAL STAFF DEVELOPMENT

Understanding teaming
Initial staff development activities should lead to a full understanding of the interdisciplinary organization and its possibilities for enhancing students, staff,

and the curriculum. Discussions ensuing from answering the following questions will help gain this needed understanding of teaming.

- What is meant by interdisciplinary teaming? How does it differ from previous attempts at team teaching?
- What possibilities does teaming create for students? for staff members? for parents? for administrators? for the curriculum?
- How are teams organized? Who designs the teams? What factors should be considered in designing teams?
- How are students assigned to teams? How are students assigned to sections within a team?
- What happens when team members do not get along with one another? Can they change teams?
- How do special education teachers relate to teams? Are they assigned to teams? How often do they meet with teams? How are their students assigned to teams?
- What is the role of the team leader? Who selects the team leader? How long should a person serve as a team leader? Are team leaders paid? If yes, how?
- How does the principal's role change when teaming is implemented? What new responsibilities does the principal have in a team organization?
- What takes place during team meetings? Should teams meet every day? How much time should be spent discussing students? instruction? curriculum?
- How are teachers assigned to teams? What are some ways this can be done?
- How are encore teachers placed on teams? What are some models indicating how this is done? Why is it important to place all teachers on teams?

- How does a team communicate with other teams? With staff members not on teams? With the administration? With parents?
- What are the costs involved with teaming? Is it more expensive? To what extent?
- What kinds of decisions do teams make that teachers have not made in the past? What problems are encountered in team decision making?
- How does teaming affect instruction? evaluation and reporting?
- What kind of staff development is necessary to make teaming effective in a middle school?
- What is the research on teaming? Do students learn better? Are teachers happy with teaming? Have schools abandoned teaming?
- What professional resources should be available for teams?
- Where can we go to see quality teams in action?

These questions face middle school staff members in their attempt to understand the concept of teaming. Because change is frightening, it is important to make it clear that teachers on teams have a great amount of autonomy in making decisions that affect them and their students. Focusing on the very real "positive possibilities" of teaming can relieve some stress that staff members have about considering this basic change in organizational structure. On the other hand, the changes required to implement teaming should not be downplayed.

Initial staff development can be accomplished by bringing knowledgeable resource persons to the school, preferably a team of teachers from a school with effective teaming, viewing videotapes, attending middle level conferences, and reading the many professional resources now available on teaming. Study groups should be formed so that discussions can continue after the general inservice meeting. These groups become means of sharing readings and results of visits, and holding informal conversations in which apprehensions can be aired.

Visiting middle schools with teaming

Early staff development plans should include visits by staff members and administrators to middle schools with effective teaming programs. Learning from fellow teachers is a powerful way to gain an understanding of teaming. It is best for a group of three or four persons including an administrator to visit any one school. The interchange among those making the visit is valuable, and their impact on the remainder of the faculty is much greater than if only one or two visited a school.

Asking the right questions will provide the right kind of information for sharing among staff members. Below are questions to guide visits to middle schools:

- How many students are in the school?
- How long has this school had teaming?
- How are the teams designed?
- Are teams designed the same way for each grade level?
- Are all teachers on teams? If so, how is this done?
- How many students are on each team?

- How are students assigned to teams?
- How are special education students and their teachers aligned with teams?
- How are team leaders selected?
- Are team leaders remunerated for responsibilities? If so, how?
- What staff development activities were provided when teaming was implemented?
- What happens when team members do not get along?
- What were teacher reactions to teaming when it was first implemented?
- What problems were encountered when teaming was implemented?
- How do you feel about teaming now? What do you like about it? What do you dislike about it?
- How has student learning benefited from teaming?
- What reactions have parents had to teaming?
- What suggestions do you have for us as we consider teaming?
- How do teams use common planning time?

All teachers and administrators should visit at least one middle school and share and discuss the visits in some formal way. If the discussion generates additional questions, or if the answers are not satisfactory, then additional study and discussion may be necessary before implementing teaming.

Developing team leadership

Strong team leadership creates high performing teams. Ideally, team leaders would receive special training before teaming is implemented. Their skills will then be a significant boost for team building and establishing consistent expectations for students.

Building the team

Helping teachers become fully functioning team members is the next staff development activity. Team building activities should be designed to answer the following questions:

- What is the difference between a group and a team?
- What are the characteristics of an effective team?
- What goals are appropriate for teams?
- What roles should be a part of each team?
- How do team members communicate with one another?
- How do team members communicate with members of other teams?
- What ground rules should be established by each team?
- How will the team make decisions, solve problems, and manage conflict?
- What stages of development do teams go through?

These items are discussed in a number of chapters as well as in this chapter.

Establishing consistent expectations for students on teams

This aspect of staff development closely follows team building. It requires teams to initiate discussions about consistent management, instructional, and learning skill expectations for students. It also provides an opportunity for team members to practice their team-building skills.

Premises for Setting Expectations: To begin this staff development activity, teams must agree on three premises:

- Each decision should be made on the basis of "What's best for kids." While decisions affect teachers, administrators, and the curriculum, the education of students must have the highest priority.
- There is more than one good way to do things. Teachers, especially those with experience, realize there are a variety of effective ways of handling items such as tardiness, late homework, and cheating. While they may be comfortable with strategies they have been using, they know other procedures can and do work effectively.
- All teachers can change and be effective. Teachers have some uneasiness, however, when they realize that when they are in concert with teammates, a new satisfaction will arise and their sense of professional accomplishment will grow.

When faculty members accept these premises, they are ready to establish tentative expectations for their students. These expectations may change as they implement them and receive feedback from students.

Team expectations for students: Three sets of expectations need to be discussed by team members.

- Classroom management procedures: These include but are not limited to the following items: tardiness, leaving the classroom, cheating, improper language, put-downs, food and drink in the classroom, required supplies, use of an organizational notebook, covering of books, writing of notes, fighting, and name calling.
- Classroom instructional procedures: These include but are not limited to the following items: grading procedures, late work, makeup work, extra credit, proficiency reports, deficiency reports, homework, and paper headings.

- Learning skills: These include but are not limited to the following items: reading, writing, speaking, listening, note taking, study skills, information retrieval, test taking, critical thinking, and organizational skills.

Worksheets for these sets of expectations are included in Chapter 15.

Establishing management and instructional expectations

The following tested procedure will work to establish management and instructional expectations.

- Select an item for discussion. Each team member explains the procedure he/she currently uses.
- After sharing these, team members must decide if students will benefit from establishing one procedure that all will follow. If they agree, as they should, that one procedure is better for students than several different procedures, they must decide which procedure to use. This means all will follow one teacher's current approach or a newly created one that is acceptable to all.
- If team members cannot reach agreement in a reasonable amount of time, the item should be put on hold and a new item considered. After all items in these first two categories have been discussed, the team should return to those items where no agreement was reached. When a team has reached agreement on some items, it is usually easier to reach agreement on the more difficult issues. If a team cannot agree to adopt a common procedure or cannot agree on a common procedure, each member will have to continue using his/her present procedure until the team revisits the issue at a later date.

Establishing consistent learning skills

The enduring importance of students possessing learning skills and being able to be lifelong learners makes this category of great importance. A procedure to follow that will establish consistency in teaching these critical learning skills follows:

- Complete an inventory of learning skills usually taught by each team member. The inventory will determine those skills emphasized in each discipline and the extent to which they are emphasized. Furthermore, developing the inventory will likely reveal skills overlooked. Chapter 15 includes an inventory form.

- After completing the inventory, each learning skill is discussed to seek consensus on such questions as the following:

  To what extent should this skill to be taught at this grade level?
  Should one member or all members teach each of the skills?
  How will this skill be taught?
  When should this skill be taught? How reinforced?

If the amount of staff development time is limited, teams should concentrate on three items: study skills, note-taking, and information retrieval. These skills should be emphasized at the beginning of the school year; therefore, team decisions on these skills should be made prior to the beginning of school. The remaining skills can be discussed during common planning time.

Team discussions on classroom management, instructional management, and learning skills usually take between 8-12 hours to complete. Providing released time for teams of teachers, if possible, is the best means to accomplish this very important task. Summer work on these items is appropriate only if all team members are present.

Team meeting activities

Participating in a common planning period is a new experience for most teachers. Therefore, it is important to consider those activities that will become a part of the daily planning period. Team meeting time is built around the following activities:

- **Student concerns:** During the first year of teaming, student learning, social development, and behavior concerns usually dominate the planning period. Teams should limit their discussion of students to no more than 30 percent of their meeting time. There is a strong tendency to focus primarily on students who are experiencing difficulties; these discussions, however, must include consideration of all students. Team leaders need to be sensitive to team members whining about student behaviors. Whining has no positive effect on students and should not be tolerated in team meetings.

- **Resource persons**: The planning period provides an excellent opportunity to communicate with various resource persons. In some middle schools, teachers of students with special needs are full-time team members. When this is not the case, these teachers should attend team meetings on a scheduled basis. The counselor may be scheduled weekly but attend only if his/her services are needed. Media personnel meet with the team monthly to discuss new materials available for instructional purposes or when a new unit is being planned. The school nurse and school psychologist are also involved as needed. The lines of communication are important if the services of resource persons are to be used during the school year.

    Some teams use common planning time for parent conferencing. While highly desirable, conferencing with parents is very labor intensive and must be restricted so teams can attend to other issues.

    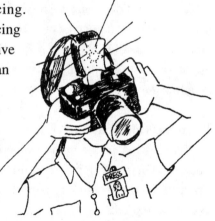

    Resource persons are valuable for teams. However, team meeting time as well as the time of the resource person is valuable and limited. Therefore, resource persons should only attend meetings on invitation.

- **Student activities:** Providing recognition, social, and recreational activities is an excellent way to create a sense of unity and belonging for students on the team. Teams can use planning time to organize activities to develop an esprit de corps.

- **Professional activities:** Teams should use at least one planning period every two weeks to discuss professional issues. A person who attended a conference could share information gleaned from the meeting. Teachers might each read a particular article at home and share reactions

during this occasional professional activity
period. A team could also decide to read
a professional book, discussing a chapter or two every two weeks. Or a team
might learn how to use a particular
computer program or piece
of technology.

• **Curriculum:** During common
planning time, team mem-
bers share topics they in-
tend to teach and what will
be required of students. Sharing requirements will alleviate uninten-
tionally overloading students with tests, projects, or homework. Sharing topics is a first step toward curriculum integration. When team
members become aware of topics taught by one another, informal cor-
relation occurs and the possibility of integration improves dramati-
cally.

Teams that have effective leadership are efficient with routine team duties and control the amount of time spent discussing student concerns so they are able to utilize planning time for curriculum
improvement. Teams should not be distressed, however, if little planning time is spent on curriculum integration during the first semester
or even year. The first year they should concentrate primarily on moving from being just a group to becoming a real team where building
collegiality and concern for students' academic and personal welfare
is present.

FOLLOW-UP STAFF DEVELOPMENT ACTIVITIES

Regardless of the amount of staff development provided when teaming is first
introduced into a middle school, it is important that teaming be continuously
monitored and additional training provided.

As noted in Chapter 5, teams in Stage One will gravitate toward the discussion of student behaviors and team housekeeping responsibilities during com-

mon planning time. Unless stimu-
lated to move beyond these two areas, teams will not utilize the full
potential inherent in teaming. Toward the end of the first year of
teaming, teams should be required
to reflect on their positive accomplishments, identify areas they feel
need attention, and determine the resources necessary to improve teaming. The survey included in Chap-

ter 14 pinpoints areas where additional staff development is necessary. Based
on the results obtained by the administration of this instrument in numerous
middle schools where teaming was in its first year as well as where teams were
in effect for a number of years, the following issues were identified most often
as needing attention.

Refocusing of team goals

Teams recognize very quickly when their major use of team planning time
consists of repeated discussions of a limited number of students along with
housekeeping duties. Such teams need to refocus their attention on goals that
will have a greater impact on all students. Staff development experiences that
allow teams to explore these conditions will be extremely valuable.

Clarifying team member roles

While agreement on ways to share the team
workload was established at the onset of teaming, it
is easy for teams to drift away from this desirable
team procedure. Having one or two people assume
almost all the responsibilities of the team or having
to identify someone to carry out a responsibility each
time an issue arises are signs of an inefficient and
somewhat dysfunctional team. Reviewing and reaffirming each member's responsibility and contribu-
tion to the team is important.

Reaffirming team ground rules

Unless team ground rules are reviewed on a continuous basis, it is easy to fall into habits detrimental to the team's functioning. Being absent or late to meetings, correcting papers during team meetings, and domination of meetings by one or two people severely limits the effectiveness of the team. Team leaders need to be sensitive to any straying from established ground rules and challenge team members to reaffirm these procedures.

A major problem confronting many middle school teams is the numerous interruptions of team planning time. A few interruptions can quickly escalate until teams have little time for important work. If teams are to operate effectively, they need to set their own agenda and not allow other personnel in the building to usurp team planning time. When this is a problem for one team, it undoubtedly is an issue with other teams as well, so team leaders and the principal should develop school-wide procedures that apply to all teams and communicate these procedures to everyone.

Decision making, problem solving, and conflict management

As detailed in Chapters 9-11, the skills of decision making, problem solving, and conflict management help distinguish high performing teams from low performing ones. When teaming is initiated, most decisions faced by the team are made with little difficulty because the decisions usually center around issues that team members are comfortable making, ones that don't bring into conflict team members' philosophies or their long-established teaching methods. As teams move into the territorial waters of curriculum and instruction, there is a greater need to focus on these three teaming skills. Staff development activities specifically devoted to these items will assist teams in functioning at a higher level.

Restructuring team planning time

Of all activities that a team can do to improve teaming, restructuring team planning time is the most important. Analyzing how time misspent in common planning activities is worth serious consideration. Prior to a discussion of this topic, it would be most useful to have each team review its team records for a period of three to four weeks to determine the amount of time spent on the different types of activities that take place during team planning time. These data often convince teams of the need to reallocate the precious time available.

Two major areas of improvement in team planning time are addressed below. Placing greater emphasis on these two items will improve the education of middle level students.

- **Interdisciplinary planning and teaching**: The advocacy of interdisciplinary and multidisciplinary units of instruction inundates the literature on teaming. Unfortunately, many teams have fallen into a trap. Most interdisciplinary units reported in the literature and taught in middle schools have three characteristics: (1) they represent curriculum beyond the normal curriculum required to be taught at that grade level, (2) they begin and end at the same time, and (3) they involve all disciplines on the team simultaneously

  As a result, teams are often stymied because these units demand considerable planning time and take team members away from what they view as "their" curriculum requirements. Furthermore, some team members may feel coerced into joining the efforts to teach an interdisciplinary unit although their discipline does not fit the theme of the unit. Staff development devoted to finding natural intersections between just *two* disciplines represented on the team offers many opportunities to create meaningful curricular connections. Sometimes these units need not be taught simultaneously. For example, the metric system might be taught in mathematics just prior to the time students are engaged in using these concepts in science. Creating units involving two disciplines and based on the required curriculum in these disciplines expands the opportunities to provide curricular connections that will benefit students.

- **Integrating technology into the curriculum**: Society is expecting technology to be incorporated into classroom instruction. But with technology growing and changing so rapidly, many teachers are becoming frustrated. They realize their obligation to utilize technology in the classroom, but learning how to operate the hardware as well as being comfortable with a wide variety of software is an overwhelming expectation. This problem provides a tremendous opportunity offered for cooperative work possible in teaming. If a team desires to maximize the use of technology in its classrooms, it makes sense for each teacher on the team to specialize in one or more areas. For example, one teacher might become the expert in the use of the Internet; another might serve the team well by specializing in desktop publishing programs, while presentation and graphics  software could be the strengths of other team members. When a teacher on the team wishes to use one of these programs such as presentation software, the team member who has expertise with this program could assist that teacher and/or could trade classes for one or more days and teach the students how to use presentation programs. Furthermore, during team planning time, each team member could "teach" others how to use the hardware and software as well as discuss strategies for incorporating technology into their instructional activities. By creating resource persons on the team, the likelihood of utilizing more technology in the instructional process is enhanced.

In Chapter 15, a survey instrument developed with the assistance of Trish Graves from Cooperative Educational Service Agency #11 in Wisconsin is presented that can be used by team members to assess their strengths in a variety of technological areas. Completing this form will provide a profile of the technological expertise on the team. This profile will help determine who is ready to serve as a technology resource person on the team and identify those areas where other members may want to serve as a resource person.

Prior to a discussion of this topic, it would be useful to have each team assess its team records for three to four weeks to determine the amount of time spent on the different types of activities that take place during team planning time. These data often convince teams of the need to reallocate the limited time available for planning.

Weekly schedule of team meeting time

A weekly or biweekly schedule of activities is imperative if teams aspire to high levels of performance. Knowing what is to occur each day reduces confusion and frustration. In Figure 35, a suggested weekly schedule is provided. Note that three days are allocated for curricular and instructional matters. To meet the intent of this schedule, teams must find ways to reduce time spent discussing the same small group of students as well as decrease time spent on housekeeping duties. This will make it possible to move forward with important curricular and instructional issues that can have a significant effect of the achievement of all student on their team. With good leadership, courage, and discipline by all members, improvements in team effectiveness can be achieved.

SUMMARY

There is no substitute for quality staff development when making the change to an interdisciplinary organizational structure within a middle school. Teaming has untold potential for improving teaching and learning and the attitudes of both teachers and students. Staff development efforts must help teachers understand the concept of teaming and its possibilities and help them learn how to become effective team members. Specific activities should be directed toward making evident the opportunities for enhancing learning within this type of organizational structure. It is imperative that the school district provide the support needed for staff development activities. To ensure a quality teaming program, more than a decision to try it and a one-day inservice program is needed. The time and money invested in staff development will pay off in faculty morale and student achievement. ❏

Figure 35
Suggested Weekly Schedule for Team Planning Time

DAY ONE
   Preview of week
   Upcoming content
   Upcoming requirements
   Social activities
   Recognitions/awards
   Parents

DAY TWO
   Discussion of selected students

   Note: The counselor or any other support personnel may be
          present if they can contribute to the discussion of the
          students under consideration

DAY THREE, FOUR, and FIVE

   Devoted to instructional and curricular matters. This may include
but not limited to the following:

   - sharing instructional strategies
   - determining connections between curricular areas and
     developing interdisciplinary approaches to meeting these
     connections
   - reviewing appropriate assessment procedures
   - developing technological approaches to enhance
     instructional strategies
   - considering procedures to meet the diverse needs of
     students on the team

   Utilize one day every two weeks for professional development

9

Team Decision Making

*Obvious advantages of a group decision-
making and problem-solving process are
that it expands the range of available
options, enhances the quality of the solutions, and increases commitment among
those involved.*   – Glenn H. Varney

T eaming in schools is a powerful organizational strategy. While much
can be accomplished by professionals working alone, more can be
gained by having people work in a collaborative mode. The results of
effective teamwork can be enormous, but the process of reaching a high level
of performance requires special skills. One of those important skills is decision
making.

Most team decisions can be made informally. However, when difficult issues arise, it is important that the team have an agreed upon decision-making
procedure in place. Making decisions is much easier when working independently. Decisions made by a team have to reflect the concerns, biases, and experiences of each member. Bridging the beliefs of each individual in order to
satisfy all involved in the decision-making process is often a difficult task.

EXAMPLES OF TEAM DECISIONS

Interdisciplinary teams make a multitude of decisions such as those below:
- Responding to the behaviors of specific students
- Providing social activities for students
- Grading and reporting procedures
- Correlating and integrating the curriculum
- Meeting the special needs of students on the team

- Teaching basic learning skills
- Responding to the concerns of other teams and faculty not on teams
- Interacting with parents of students on the team
- Integrating technology into instruction
- Completing a team service project

CONSENSUS DECISION MAKING

Attempting to reach a decision that will satisfy all members of a team is termed *consensus decision making*. Reaching consensus requires everyone to voluntarily accept and support the final decision. While some members may not be completely satisfied with the decision, they agree to support it.

Fortunately, most decisions by middle school teams can be reached satisfactorily without going through the full consensus procedure. Consensus decision making can be a long, thoughtful process. Time spent in making the decision is offset, however, by greater satisfaction and agreement in the implementation of the decision.

The following principles must be followed to reach consensus.

- Each person must fully understand the items being discussed.
- Each person must be frank in expressing his/her view. No hidden agendas are allowed.
- Views, even if unpopular, must be heard thoughtfully, thoroughly, and without prejudice.
- Each person must listen actively, discuss openly, and be creative in his/her thinking.
- Each person must think and act beyond selfish interests, placing the welfare of the team first.

There are two major components of consensus decision making. First, generating potential solutions to the issues at hand, and second, determining which of the proposals seem best and can be supported by all team members.

Step One: Brainstorming

Brainstorming is a process used to generate the maximum number of ideas or possible solutions to a problem. If done well, a lengthy and creative list of items emerges, one or more of which may be acceptable and supportable by all team members. In order to achieve this result, certain rules apply to the brain-storming process.

- When generating ideas, no member of the team may make value judg-ments about thoughts rendered by a member. Only when there is a perceived freedom to put forth any idea however unrelated and foolish it may seem, is there a chance to generate the most creative ideas and possible solutions. Value judgments may be made later in the decision-making process, but not now.

- Quantity is more important than quality. The more ideas generated, the greater the opportunity for an acceptable and supportable solution.

- Creativity is a crucial goal of the brainstorming process. Seemingly wild and crazy ideas should be encouraged as a means of generating a quantity of ideas from which a quality solution can emerge. It is acceptable to piggyback on someone's idea.

The brainstorming process can be conducted by allowing team members to randomly put forth ideas, or it can be done in a round robin fashion after members have generated their own list. The latter assures all members will be involved in the process whereas the former may result in some members dominating the process.

When the team members appear to run out of ideas, the focus of the session changes to determine if there are any duplicate items or if confusing items need to be clarified. No effort should be made to promote or criticize items on the list at this point.

(Note to the team leader for Step One: remind all team members of the ground rules to eliminate unacceptable verbal and nonverbal comments during the brainstorming; decide whether to follow a random or round robin process; when Step One is finished, clean up the list by eliminating duplicates or confusing items.)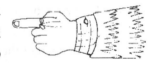

Step Two: Reducing the brainstormed list

The second step is to reduce the many suggestions to a manageable number usually in the range of 3-5 items Several techniques to achieve this step are described below.

- Multi-voting: In multi-voting, members of the team select their top choices from the total list. The number of choices is somewhat arbitrary but may depend on the length of the list. This will produce a set of items receiving significant number of votes and identify those items receiving few or no votes. After some discussion, a second round of voting further reduces the number of ideas. Voting and discussion can continue until the same items receive the same number of votes.

Example of Multi-Voting

An eighth grade team is attempting to identify
a service project for its team

Step 1:   *The team brainstorms 30 service projects; they reduce this*
          list to five or fewer items.
Step 2:   *They agree that, in the first round of voting, members will*
          select their top ten projects, and items receiving two or no
          votes will be deleted from the list.
Step 3:   *The voting is done and the results tallied and discussed.*
Step 4:   *Steps two and three are repeated until the same items re-*
          ceive the same number of votes.

- Nominal group technique: This technique requires team members to select their top choices from the list but also to prioritize the items selected. If each member selects four items from the brainstormed list, then each of the four items is rated one to four with four indicating the highest priority. This will produce a reduced list and identify the priority of each of the items selected.

- Dot technique: This technique, a variation of the nominal group procedure, entails developing a selected list of items from the master list that indicates the priorities of the choices. *Stick-em* dots of different colors are used, each color representing a different value. Members "spend" their dots on ideas and values are totaled.

(Note to team leader for Step Two: review the selected procedure for reducing the number of brainstormed choices; help team members to work independently so as not to influence others; help the team decide which items remain in the potential solutions list; be sensitive to team members desiring a quick decision.)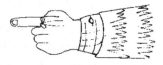

Example of Nominal Group Technique

*A seventh-grade team is attempting to identify
a field trip for its team*

Step 1: The team brainstorms sixteen possible field trips. They decide to reduce the number to four.

Step 2: On a sheet of paper, identify each of the sixteen items by the letter A, B, C, etc.

Step 3: Each member selects four items from the list of sixteen and places the letter of that item on a slip of paper.

Step 4: The four items selected are ranked from four to one (highest ranked item receives a four, the next a three, etc.) and the ranking placed on the slip of paper.

Step 5: Using the master list of items, obtain the ranking from each team member. Place on the master list and add up the ranking points. For example, item A may have received ranking points of 3, 2, and 4 for a total of 9; item B ranking points of 1 and 3 for a total of 4.

Step 6. Determine which items have the highest rating. Discuss the results and do the procedure again to reduce the number further if necessary.

If after the first round using the dot technique, nominal group technique, or multivoting, there exists a wide range of items beyond the desired 3-5 items, it is permissible to repeat the process keeping only those items that received some votes from the first procedure. If this does not produce the desired short list, it may be necessary to keep a larger number of items for the next step in the consensus process. Try very hard to keep people from becoming impatient at this point in the process.

Step Three: Listing the positive and negative aspects of each item

Each of the items in the short list is systematically studied by team members. Both the positive and negative aspects of the items are identified. While this step may take time, it is important that all members be involved. Some

Example of the Dot Technique

A sixth-grade team is attempting to identify
a set of goals for its team for the ensuing school year.

Step 1: The team brainstorms a number of items.

Step 2: Each member receives three stick-em dots, one blue, one red, one yellow. A red dot equals three points, blue equals two, and yellow equals one.

Step 3: Team members "spend" their three dots by placing them on the master list of brainstormed goals. If a person feels strongly about one item, all three dots can be placed on that item, or the three dots can be spread over three items.

Step 4: Tally the value of the dots placed on each item.

Step 5: Discuss the results; repeat the dot procedure to reduce the number further if needed. All items receiving at least one red dot (someone's highest ranking) should remain on the list for further discussion and voting.

team members may want to use this time to lobby for support of certain items. The team leader needs to be sensitive to this and keep the discussion moving without offending any of the participants.

(Note to team leader for Step Three: discuss the positive and negative aspects of each item; keep lobbying by team members to a minimum.)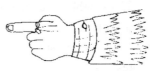

Step Four: Making feelings known about each item

This is a sensitive step but extremely important to the process. All members are asked by the team leader to indicate their feelings about each item. Members are not allowed to pass on an item, but it is appropriate to indicate they have neutral feelings on certain items.

(Note to team leader for Step Four: review the process with team members; try to keep the conversa-
tion moving without offending individuals. It may
be appropriate to set a time limit for each item es-
pecially if one or more team members are known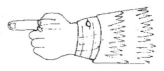
for their skills of elucidation on topics of importance to them; be sure that each
team member expresses his/her feelings.)

Step Five: Checking for consensus

After looking at the positive and negative attributes of each item under consideration and ascertaining the feelings of each member on each item, the discussion may have reached a point to determine if consensus is possible. Often
times, groups will conduct a "straw vote" to learn the direction members are
leaning.

Writers on consensus decision making have different views on what procedure to follow next. Some thoughts on various scenarios are described below.

- If no solution is evident, "practical consensus" should be called into
  play and a vote taken to determine the course of action.

- If two items receive high support from all team members, the issue of
  using both should be considered. Should this not be applicable to the
  decision being made, further discussion may pinpoint the better solution of the two. If it is not appropriate to consider both, then one might
  be put off for future utilization.

- If no item has significant support by the majority of team members, the
  team is best advised to begin the process over starting with the brainstorming activity. If this process fails to produce a supportable solution, the team may wish to forego the issue under consideration.

- If one member is a blocker to a collaborative decision, the team may
  ask that person to "stand aside" and allow remaining members to reach
  a consensus. This could allow a team to pilot an idea with the hope that
  it will be successful and the blocker will agree to participate.

- Should a team continually be unable to reach consensus on a variety of issues, the team may wish to move to the conflict resolution procedures described in Chapter 11.

EXAMPLE OF CONSENSUS DECISION MAKING

A seventh-grade team is attempting to reach consensus on a service project.

Step 1: The team brainstormed the following items:

    A. Helping the elderly by raking leaves, etc.
    B. Tutoring elementary students
    C. Picking up road garbage
    D. Working in the library
    E. Thanksgiving/Christmas food drives
    F. Visiting adults in nursing homes
    G. Assisting disabled students
    H. Helping the family with home chores
    I. Peer tutoring
    J. Cleaning up the school property

Step 2: They decide to reduce the number to at least four. Each member selects four items from the list of ten and places the letter of that item on a slip of paper.

Step 3: The four items selected by each team member are ranked from four to one (highest ranked item receives a four, the next a three, etc.) and the ranking placed on the corresponding slip of paper.

Step 4: Using the master list of items, obtain the rankings from each team member. Place on the master list and add up the ranking points. The chart below shows the ranking points for each item.

A.	Helping the elderly by raking leaves, etc.	15
B.	Tutoring elementary students	2
C.	Pick up road garbage	0
D.	Work in the library	2
E.	Thanksgiving/Christmas food drives	10
F.	Visiting adults in nursing homes	0
G.	Assisting disabled students	2
H.	Helping the family with home chores	0
I.	Peer tutoring	1
J.	Cleaning up the school property	8

Step 5: Determine which items have the highest rating. From the rankings, it is evident that item A, E, and J will remain in the list of potential service projects.

Step 6: List the positive and negative aspects of each of the remaining items.

A. Helping the elderly by raking leaves and related yard work.
   Positive:
      Teaches concern for elderly people
      Can be done throughout the school year
   Negative:
      Students will need to be transported to work places

E. Thanksgiving/Christmas food drives
   Positive:
      Are of short duration
   Negative:
      Will need to have students solicit donations

J. Cleaning up the school property
Positive:
Sense of ownership for students
Easily assessable for students
Negative:
None given

Step 7: The team leader leads a discussion on the feelings of each team member on each of the three items.

Step 8: A straw vote is taken and it appears that all team members feel most positive about item J – *cleaning up the school property*. Based on this show of support, this item was selected as the first service project for the seventh grade class.

USING CONSENSUS DECISION MAKING

Consensus decision making is an attempt to help all team members to reach quality and important decisions. As with other forms of decision making, it must be used at appropriate times.

- When to use:
  -issues impact everyone on the team
  -issues that require commitment and ownership of the entire team

- When not to use:
  -in a crisis situation because it takes so much time
  -not enough technical information to make a good decision

CONSENSUS DECISION MAKING AND THE TEAM LEADER

Consensus decision making is a process that requires effective leadership in order to reach the high level of support desired. The team leader needs to be aware of team member feelings about decision making and those issues in which team members desire to be involved. Knowing the skill level of team members to successfully navigate collaborative decision making is important. And discerning how much time team members are willing to devote to consensus decision making is crucial for the team leader.

SUMMARY

Teachers can come to agreement on most simple items without using any formal decision-making procedure. However, team members should be skilled in decision making for those few difficult decisions. Becoming good decision makers takes study and practice. If interdisciplinary teams in middle level schools are to move to a higher level of efficiency and effectiveness, the skill of consensus decision making should be learned and used. ❏

10

Team Problem Solving

*Too often solutions are applied without thoroughly
knowing the problem, or the symptom of the
problem rather than the problem itself is attacked.*

— Joseph C. Fields

Middle school teams encounter problems that need resolution in such areas as the following:

- students – resolving the issue of frequent absences or continually missing assignments
- communication – connecting with some parents about the progress of their children
- curriculum – agreeing on the extent and form of thematic units
- instruction – meeting the needs of students with a wide range of abilities and interests
- organization – eliminating tracking on teams.

Teams in the initial stage of formation may struggle with a process to resolve such issues while mature teams have developed a problem-solving process that can be applied to any situation facing the team. Teams that are comfortable with a process will not fear problems but will systematically apply the process and continue their work without allowing an issue to create dissension.

The problem-solving process is quite generic. Most writers on the topic agree that the process involves five steps.

Step One: Define the problem

The first and most important step is to define the problem clearly. On the surface this may appear to be a relatively simple step. Yet, unless the problem is succinctly defined, a team may end up with a great solution to a different problem. It is, therefore, essential for the team to respond to such questions as the following:

- How does each of us define the problem?
- How often is the problem occurring and under what circumstances?
- What information do we have about the causes of the problem?
- Who is affected and to what extent?

To define the problem is to look beyond the symptoms to uncover the "real" problem. For example, a team concerned about the number of missing assignments, after investigation discovers that the student's assignments are missing only the Fridays and Mondays when the youngster spends a weekend with his/her non-custodial parent. Thus, the real problem to be resolved is how to ensure that homework is completed on days surrounding those weekends or how  to make adjustments in the requirements. It is helpful if team members are aware of tools available to help define the true causes of a problem. These tools are described later in this chapter. Once the problem has been clearly defined, the team is ready to move on to the next step.

Step Two: Identify solutions

The more potential solutions identified to resolve a problem, the better the chances that the solution selected will be an effective one. To ensure a lengthy list of potential solutions to the problem, the team might invite others such as the school nurse, guidance counselor, and attendance officer to be involved in this process. The knowledge and unique experiences of these people can assist the team in finding creative solutions.

Continuing the example of the student who is missing assignments after spending a weekend with a non-custodial parent, the counselor, social worker, and perhaps both parents would be able to generate worthwhile solutions. Often the student will have ideas that should be considered. Brainstorming within the team and/or with resource people is an excellent way to generate possible solutions.

Step Three: Evaluate and select the best solution

Prior to choosing the best solution, it is imperative that the criteria for the solution be defined. Questions that guide this discussion are

- Will it have a long-term effect on the problem, or is it just a short-term solution?
- Can the solution be managed by the team, or is it beyond the expertise of the team?
- What time limits are imposed on the solution?
- What resources are needed to implement the solution, and will these resources be available?
- Will the solution be an acceptable one for members of the team and any other people who are involved?
- What are the risks involved in a particular solution?
- Does a particular solution create additional problems?

When the criteria have been established, the team begins the decision-making process including brainstorming, reducing the number of solutions, and selecting the best one.

Step Four: Implement the selected decision

It will be advantageous if all members have agreed upon the solution, because all must be involved in implementing the decision. Making sure that all members understand their roles in carrying out the solution will reduce the possibility for confusion. The timeline for implementation must be developed to ensure a logical and effective movement toward a resolution. Finally, the procedures for evaluating the progress of the resolution must be selected so that important data can be collected.

Step Five: Evaluate the solution and adjust

This step includes collecting data on the progress of the resolution, evaluating the data, and making necessary adjustments in the process. Teams may consider using one or more of the following problem-solving tools to collect and analyze the data.

PROBLEM-SOLVING TOOLS

The steps of defining the problem and evaluating the solution rest on collecting and analyzing data. These latter two items are often treated lightly or disregarded when attempting to resolve problems, yet they yield essential information that can have a very positive effect on identifying and implementing solutions. Various procedures can be used to collect and analyze data. Some emphasize the collection of data, others the analysis of data, and many foster both collection and analysis. In the sections that follow, a number of problem-solving tools are described with information on their use, together with examples where appropriate and indications on when the particular tool would be most appropriate to use.

AFFINITY DIAGRAM

An affinity diagram is a technique to generate a number of ideas and place them in similar groupings. Ordering random data will bring an issue into focus. While the affinity diagram does not solve a problem, it will help in the process. This technique can be used with any brainstorming activity.

Developing an affinity diagram

Once a team has identified a topic to be brainstormed, index cards or sticky notes are provided to record items, one to a card. When the brainstorming is completed and all items clarified, the cards or notes are placed on a wall or flat surface and sorted by the participants. Done in silence, items are placed in groups where there seems to be a relationship between the items. Header cards are designed for each group. When only one item exists in a group, some attempt should be made to place this item with another group.

Potential affinity diagram examples

Brainstorming problems exhibited by students on the team
Brainstorming types of awards for student work

BRAINSTORMING

Brainstorming, described in detail in Chapter 9, will elicit lots of ideas from members of a group.

Potential brainstorming examples
Generating ideas for thematic units
Determining alternative ways to handle particular discipline problems
Making a list of places to take students on a field trip.

CHECKLIST

A checklist is designed to record the presence or absence of an item or process. It should be designed so that data can be collected with a minimum of effort yet result in a consistent process.

Using a checklist
A checklist will ensure consistency in data collection. For example, no steps will be overlooked when planning a field trip. The team will not have to develop all steps each time the process is implemented, thus speeding up the planning process. A checklist can be developed by discussing all steps in a process and then clarifying and eliminating duplicates. It can be validated by using it in a simulated example or a real situation. See Figure 36.

Potential checklist examples
Planning an award ceremony
Student participation in team activities
Steps in student projects
Participation in class
Parent participation in school activities

Figure 36

Field Trip Planning Checklist

		YES	NO
1.	Reached team agreement on date of field trip	____	____
2.	Reached team agreement on destination	____	____
3.	Planned classroom preparation to make the field trip educationally worthwhile	____	____
4.	Budget sufficient to make the trip	____	____
5.	Cleared with administration	____	____
6.	Proper notification of parents	____	____
7.	Transportation planned	____	____
8.	Parent consent forms designed and distributed	____	____
9.	Arrangements made for lunch and dinner	____	____
10.	Emergency plans in place	____	____
11.	Planned appropriate follow-up activities	____	____

FISHBONE DIAGRAM

A fishbone diagram is a graphic display of the causes for a particular problem. It is so named because, when developed, it resembles the spine of a fish. Based on an analysis of the graphical display of information obtained by brainstorming, it is easier to determine a procedure for addressing causes of the problem.

Constructing a fishbone diagram

1. Gain agreement on the issue under consideration.
2. Identify the major categories of concerns. Examples are people, methods, materials, resources, building, and environment. Create as many as needed. Connect these ribs to the backbone of the fishbone chart.
3. For each category, brainstorm causes of the issue under discussion and place those items on the appropriate ribs. Sometimes it is effective to brainstorm the entire list of causes before placing them on the chart. Also, some causes may fit on more than one rib.

4. Analyze the information on the fishbone to determine those causes that appear in several locations. If it is necessary to select one cause, use the procedures outlined in Chapter 9.

Potential fishbone diagram examples

Analyzing the reasons for late or missing homework
Determining why students are continuously late for class
Determining reasons for student disinterest in school
Understanding causes of student difficulty with academic subjects
Determining the causes for certain student behaviors
Finding reasons for teacher tardiness to team meetings

Example of a fishbone diagram

An example of a fishbone diagram is provided in Figure 37. The issue in this example is determining the causes of misbehavior when students are sent to the library. After completing the diagram, it would appear that the major cause for student misbehavior centers around the problems with resources available to students. The fishbone diagram helps to identify the causes of this problem.

Figure 37

Fishbone Diagram

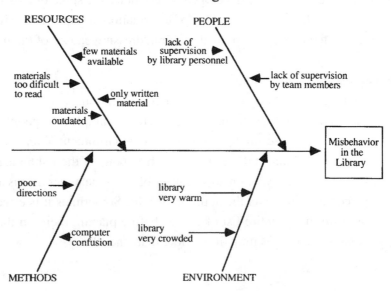

FORCED FIELD

Forced field analysis helps identify the forces that drive two sides of an issue. Viewing both the driving and restraining forces assists with strengthening the driving and reducing the restraining forces.

Designing a forced field analysis

To complete the forced field analysis, follow the steps below.

1. Draw a "T" on a large piece of newsprint. Above the horizontal line, write the goal or desired change.
2. Above the horizontal line and above the left portion of the "T," write "Driving Forces" and on the right "Restraining Forces."
3. Brainstorm a list of all possible driving and restraining forces.
4. When all items have been listed, focus the discussion on eliminating the restraining forces. Rather than strengthening the driving forces, movement toward the goal can be facilitated by reducing, eliminating, or accommodating the restraining forces.

Example of a forced field analysis

Figure 38 is an example of a forced field analysis

Figure 38

Forced Field Analysis

Driving Forces	Restraining Forces
Research doesn't support tracking	Meets the needs of gifted students
Unequal treatment of students	Meets the needs of students who learn slowly
Results in dumbed down curriculum for slower sections	The way it has always been done
No leaders in some classes	High school demands it
Harder to teach	Easier to teach
Many parents don't like it	
Some parents like it	
Makes scheduling very difficult	

MAPPING

Familiar to most teachers, this procedure provides a pictorial view of a large number of ideas and the relationship of those ideas to one another. This tool provides visualization to a brainstorming exercise. Seeing the new ideas and their relationships to others can help a team as it collects data about a particular issue.

Using a mapping activity

The main topic to be brainstormed is placed in a circle in the center of a blackboard or large sheet of paper. Individuals can then identify items related to the main idea and those items are placed in another circle with a line drawn from the new idea to the central idea. This process is continued until all ideas have been exhausted. An alternative mapping activity is to develop a timeline of topics taught during a school year. When this is done with several disciplines represented on a team, a pictorial view is provided that helps identify connecting points within the curricular areas.

Example of a mapping exercise

An example of a mapping activity is shown below.

Figure 39
Mapping

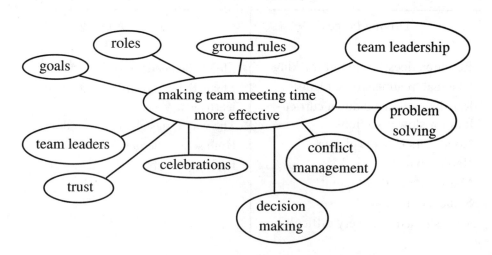

Potential mapping examples
> Developing an integrated unit of instruction
> Developing a set of activities for instructional contracts

PARETO CHARTS

A Pareto Chart is a form of a bar graph that ranks the data showing items that occur most frequently. This type of chart would help a team decide which data have the greatest impact on the issue.

Designing a Pareto Chart

A Pareto Chart displays data in graphic form showing the frequency of each set of data. It indicates the relative importance of each category and helps the viewer focus on those items having the greatest influence on the data—the vital few. To create a Pareto Chart

1. Construct a bar graph with categories on the horizontal axis and frequency on the vertical axis, and then
2. Place the category with the greatest frequency on the left and continue to the category with the smallest frequency on the right.

When graphed, it is easy to determine the category that contributes most to the problem or solution. Variations include graphing the data before and after a change in a process or break any category into sub-units forming linked Pareto Charts.

Example of a Pareto Chart

An example is shown in Figure 40. Data collected represent referrals to the office during the eight periods of the day. From the Pareto Chart, it is easy to see that most referrals come from period four, just before lunch, next highest is the last period of the day with the least number of referrals coming in period one.

Potential Pareto Chart examples

> Determining the major cause or causes of late homework
> Analyzing the reading abilities of students on the team

Figure 40
Pareto Chart

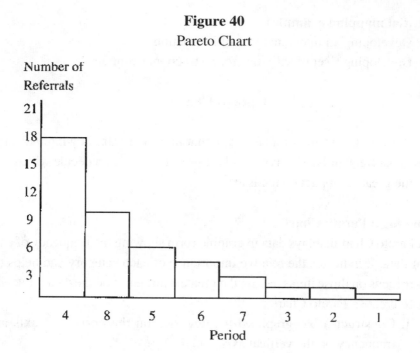

Number of
Referrals

QUESTIONNAIRES

Questionnaires or other survey instruments are used to collect data from a large group of people.

Designing a questionnaire

Designing a questionnaire may seem relatively simple, but if the results of the questionnaire are to be valid, there are a number of items that need to be considered when developing one.

- Each item must pertain directly to the subject of the questionnaire
- Each item must be written at the level of the intended audience
- Each item must focus on only one concept
- Directions must provide accurate and easy to understand information for respondents
- The instrument should be piloted on a small number of respondents to gain information on readability and consistency

Example of a Questionnaire

Figure 41 is an example of a questionnaire.

Figure 41
Questionnaire

For each item, you are to indicate the degree to which this factor is characteristic of your middle level school.

A. Significant degree   C. Slight degree   E. Do not know
B. Moderate degree   D. Not at all

In our middle level school...

_____ 1. The clubs and activities that students can join are based on
            student interests
_____ 2. The activity program helps students meet and get along with
            other students
_____ 3. Boys and girls have an equal chance to participate in clubs
            and activities
_____ 4. Everyone gets a chance to participate
_____ 5. Students are not cut from activities
_____ 6. Joining clubs and activities helps students learn how to be leaders
_____ 7. Clubs and activities take place during the school day as well as
            before and after school
_____ 8. All clubs and activities emphasize good sportsmanship
_____ 9. There are enough materials and equipment for all clubs
            and activities
_____10. There are as many activities for girls as there are for boys

Potential questionnaire topics

Student perceptions of projects, field trips, team procedures,
and celebration activities

Parents' perceptions of team activities

RUN CHARTS

A Run Chart helps to determine trends over a period of time. Data are graphed within a time period to determine changes in a process or help team members predict future occurrences of an item.

Example of a Run Chart

An example of a Run Chart is shown in Figure 42.

Figure 42

Run Chart

Teachers notice that a student is failing to complete his assignments. Generally, the boy's behavior in school seems to be very normal. To solve this problem, a team looks for the cause. The following information was collected.

Days assignment turned in:
April 1,2,3,4,10,11,12,15,16,17,23,24,25,26,29,30 May 1,2,7,8,9,10

Plot the data on a run chart to help in the process of determining the cause(s) for missing assignments by placing an X on the line for those dates that the student did <u>not</u> turn in his assignments.

```
April 1 2 3 4 5   8 9 10 11 12   15 16 17 18 19  22 23 24 25 26
        x   x x                   x       x   x
```

```
April  29 30  May 1 2 3  6 7 8 9 10
              x   x
```

Viewing the Run Chart suggests the student fails to complete assignments on days surrounding alternate weeks, this suggesting perhaps the student may be visiting a non-custodial parent.

Potential Run Chart examples
> Attendance of designated students
> Referrals to the counselor, administration, and nurse
> Lunchroom issues

SUMMARY

Effective teams develop procedures that assist them when there is a need to resolve difficult problems. Too often, problems are hurriedly decided resulting in no gains, short-term gains, or exacerbation of the problem. Developing a decision-making and problem-solving process that all team members understand and support goes a long way in helping team members achieve confidence in their ability to resolve difficult issues. Problem solving tools will help teams make wise decisions when based on adequate data. Defining the problem, identifying solutions, evaluating and selecting the best solution, implementing the decision, evaluating the solutions, and adjusting are the steps that all teams must master to be effective. ❑

11

Conflict Management

*When team members collaborate, they are
able to consider the full range of alterna-
tives, similarities, and differences; become
more clearly focused; and resolve problems
more satisfactorily.*

— Jerry Spiegel and Cresencio Torres

Conflict within a team is inevitable if the team is a growing, thriving unit. Conflict can be positive, allowing team members to explore new ideas and test opinions. Effective teams are not afraid of conflicting opinions; they realize benefits can arise from them. However, unnecessary and excessive conflict can drain team members' energies. If conflict brings such tension to the team that performance is affected, it must be resolved.

DEFINITION OF CONFLICT

Robert Maddox (1992) claims: "...conflict is present because of: differences in needs, objectives, and values; differences in perceiving motives, words, actions, and situations; differing expectations of outcomes – favorable versus unfavorable; unwillingness to work through issues, collaborate, or compromise." Conflict, then, can arise from many sources; it revolves around differences between two parties. When it results in those parties considering new ideas as they work collaboratively through their differences, conflict can be positive. However, when the differences are so severe that neither is able to consider the other's viewpoint, conflict can be destructive. It is important to understand that conflict is not inherently destructive; the problem occurs when individuals or groups are unable to handle it.

SOURCES OF CONFLICT

There are numerous examples of potential conflict within teams. A partial list is provided below.

- One core team versus another in an openly competitive way
- Team plans conflict with departmental plans
- New teachers on team versus expectations of remaining team members
- Newly assigned team leader versus expectations of team members
- Regular education teachers and special education teachers
- Integration of subject matter
- Grading procedures
- Discipline procedures

CONDITIONS FOR CONFLICT

Being aware of conditions that might create a conflict and controlling them to the greatest extent possible can help teams reduce the impact of conflict.

- If a team does not have established goals or the goals are ambiguous, members will likely establish their own goals or attempt to unilaterally set goals for the team. Keeping the team goals in clear focus by revisiting them on a regular basis will help and reduce the opportunity for conflict.
- The team is unable to make effective decisions and solve problems. Decisions may be delayed or made in a haphazard fashion to team members' dismay. Without an established process for decision making and problem solving, teams may have difficulty broaching any sensitive issues.
- Ineffective communication exists. Hiding true feelings, hesitancy when speaking, blaming others, hidden agendas, outright name calling, and using put-downs are prime examples of communication difficulties that set the stage for serious conflicts.
- Team members are unwilling to carry out their responsibilities.

- Team leadership is ineffective. Without the direction and support provided by an effective team leader, teams may lose focus and turn their energies inward against one another.

Team leaders must be cognizant of the characteristics of dysfunctional teams (see Chapter 12) paying close attention to any negative activity to ensure that it does not escalate to a significant level. Team members may, almost without realizing it, begin to polarize themselves and engage in competitive rather than cooperative activities. As conflict grows, the emotional level increases making resolution more difficult. Communication lines may be cut resulting in conflict escalation. It is more productive for a team to spend its energy creating a positive climate than to deal with the destructive consequences of conflict.

STRATEGIES FOR DEALING WITH CONFLICT

Individuals as well as teams use a variety of strategies to deal with conflict. The strategy selected will depend on the concern individuals have for maintaining a positive relationship and the concern the individuals have for achieving a particular goal. Five strategies are described below with examples and a list of advantages and disadvantages.

Avoiding

When the strategy of avoiding is in effect, team members simply choose to ignore or deny that a problem exists. They refrain from any discussion of the conflict, even though strong feelings may be present. Avoiding is often used by people who do not believe they have the ability to do anything about the conflict. In teams, members may put up with conflicts that they consider minor or unresolvable.

Examples of avoidance may include
- Putting up with annoying behavior such as a member's being late or frequently leaving team meetings early
- Carrying out other team member's responsibilities without mentioning it
- Accepting blame for others so the issues appear not to need resolution

Advantages of avoidance:
- Feelings of other people will not be hurt if the issue is not discussed
- Withdrawing from pursuing a resolution to a conflict may reduce stress
- It will be accepted as a reasonable solution when a person or group does not know how to resolve the conflict
- When an issue is not confronted, it will give the appearance that all is well within the team

Disadvantages of avoidance:
- A conflict not resolved will fester and may resurface at a later date with greater intensity
- Knowing that a conflict exists and is not being addressed will increase the internal stress of some team members
- There is no growth by the team when problems are not resolved

Leaving a conflict unresolved suggests that team members do not believe an accepted goal will be furthered by facing a conflict directly. In addition, an individual may fear disrupting existing relationships so it is easier and more comfortable to do nothing.

Smoothing

When both parties agree to disagree, they have selected a strategy known as smoothing. This strategy is utilized when preserving a working relationship with team members is of real importance. Some personal or team goals are less important than the positive feelings among team members, so why discuss the conflict if it may ruin existing positive relationships?

Some examples of smoothing are:
- Not pushing to develop consistent team expectations for students because team members manage their classroom and instruction in different ways
- Failing to work effectively with special education teachers due to an unwillingness to discuss how this might be done effectively
- Agreeing to allow some team members to teach an interdisciplinary unit without involving another member

Advantages of smoothing:
- Maintains friendships among team members
- A quick way to bypass an issue rather than spending time finding a solution
- Keeps the stress factor down when team members recognize they can avoid open discussion of topics if conflicting views exist

Disadvantages of smoothing:
- Potentially creative solutions are lost when the issue is not confronted
- Internal stress felt by team members may persist because the issue was not resolved
- The trust level between team members does not grow.

Forcing

This procedure is used when one side has a need to win at all costs. Relationships mean very little; achieving one's goal is of prime importance and getting anything less is seen as a weakness. Forcing focuses on achieving the goal even at the expense of relationships.

Examples of forcing:
- One or two team members demand that everyone on the team engage in an interdisciplinary unit

- Some team members demand that their procedure for grading be accepted as the team's position
- One or more team members continually correct papers during team meetings

Advantages of forcing:
- It results in a quick decision
- It feeds the ego of the member who is forcing the issue although it gives that person license to repeat this behavior

Disadvantages of forcing:
- The commitment to finding solutions by all team members is low
- The trust level between team members goes down
- The solutions may be less creative
- Team member relationships are very poor

Problem solving

Problem solving requires people to cooperate in serious discussions in order to reach a mutually agreeable solution. Team members agree to discuss an issue with the hope of finding a solution that will be supported by all team members. It calls for each team member to consider the ideas of others as valuable and legitimate, and it requires the skills of listening and decision making. A conflict resolved through problem solving will maintain high relationships among team members while at the same time achieving a mutual goal for the team.

Examples of problem solving on a team:
- Developing one common strategy to use with grading and reporting
- Determining whether to launch a service learning project
- Establishing consistent behavioral expectations for students

Advantages of problem solving:
- Maintains high relationships between team member
- Can result in creative and acceptable solutions
- All members of the team "win"

Disadvantages of problem solving:
  • Takes more time to reach a solution than other strategies
  • Requires special skills of all team members including the team leader

PROCESS OF PROBLEM SOLVING

When conflict exists, each party assumes a certain posture on the issue with its stance predicated on serving personal needs, values, concerns, and/or interests. If left unattended positions become more steeled, increasing the difficulty of resolving the conflict. The focus of conflict resolution should be on the underlying needs, values, concerns, and interests rather than the initial stance each party has taken on the issue. Redefining the conflict so mutual gains can be achieved by both parties becomes the goal of the resolution process (Chang, 1994; Fisher & Ury, 1983; Johnson & Johnson, 1987; Kayser, 1994; Maddux, 1992; Raider, 1992; Zander, 1994).

Because this strategy has the greatest potential for achieving team goals and maintaining positive relationships between team members, a process for problem solving is described in some detail.

Step One: Clarify the problem
Example 1: Two team members may want the team to take a field trip while the other two don't want to take a field trip

Example 2: One member may want to use portfolios as part of the assessment process while the remaining members do not.

Step Two: Identify the needs, values, and interests of both sides
Example 1: Taking a field trip may connect the curriculum to activities beyond the classroom, but it takes time away from the coverage demands of the curriculum.

Example 2: The team member interested in using portfolios may want the assessment procedures more closely tied to instructional objectives while those opposed are uncomfortable making changes from the current practices.

Step Three: Redefine the conflict to satisfy the needs of both parties

Example 1: Can a procedure be found that connects the instructional objectives beyond the classroom without creating undue pressure on completing the curriculum?

Example 2: Can an alternative assessment procedure be identified that is comfortable to all team members?

Step Four: Enter into a problem-solving procedure.

Consensus decision making, as described in Chapter 9, has the possibility of satisfying the needs of both parties. It includes brainstorming potential solutions, reducing them to a manageable number, identifying the advantages and disadvantages of each, determining each person's feelings to the potential solutions, and then selecting one solution that is acceptable and supportable by all members.

Compromise

Compromising is a strategy that allows both parties to achieve a portion of their goals and simultaneously maintain a positive relationship. Neither party is completely satisfied with the decision, but the problem is resolved and the team can move ahead.

Some examples of compromising are:
- Setting a limited number of common expectations for students as long as each team member maintains some prerogatives for dealing with students
- Agreeing to mainstream students with learning disabilities as long as students with emotional disabilities are not included
- Agreeing to heterogeneous grouping as long as one section of students is grouped in an algebra course

Advantages of compromising:
- Relationships tend to remain at a reasonably positive level.
- While the solution agreed on may not be the best, it is better than not coming to any solution whatsoever
- It represents some growth in conflict resolution on the part of the team

Disadvantages:
- While it appears that each side gained something, in reality each side lost something as well
- Continually compromising may become a typical team response to resolving issues rather than seeking a creative solution to the problem

EXAMPLE OF MANAGING CONFLICT ON A TEAM

To understand how conflict on a team might be managed, the following scenario will amplify the steps of conflict resolution.

Scenario

The seventh grade Maroon Team consists of five members. In its third year as a team, a major conflict has arisen regarding the development of interdisciplinary units of instruction. Teachers K and L want the team to cooperate on a seven-day unit on the environment. Teachers R and S are vehemently opposed to this idea. The team leader, who is committed to integration of subject matter, believes it is necessary to resolve this conflict because of its long-term effect on team activities.

The team leader looks carefully at all possible strategies to resolving the conflict.

1. Avoidance
   Avoiding this issue is no longer acceptable since this contentious issue is causing undue stress. Knowing that a lack of resolution will continue hard feelings between these two factions on the team, she feels it is necessary to consider another strategy.

2. Smoothing

   This was the procedure that the team agreed to during the first year of teaming. Because all members felt that there were so many other decisions to be made, addressing the larger issue of curriculum integration was delayed. At the beginning of the second year, the issue was resurrected and the course of action chosen was to continue to agree to disagree. Because the team leader is seeking to resolve this issue and reducing the underlying stress on the team, smoothing is not the strategy to use in resolving this team's particular conflict.

3. Forcing

   The team leader is aware that if she asks the team to discuss the issue and vote on it, whatever movement might be made toward integration will be mitigated by a lack of commitment from two members. Moreover, being forced by voting to accept the team decision will cause further alienation and continue the high level of stress on the team.

4. Compromising

   The team leader is hoping for a creative solution to this issue so a similar procedure can be used with future issues. Realizing that compromising may result in a plausible solution to this problem, she decides to first make an attempt to find a creative solution through problem solving.

5. Problem solving

   The team leader believes that problem solving has the most potential to resolve this conflict. If an agreeable and supportable solution cannot be reached by the team, then perhaps a compromise would be appropriate.

   Based on this analysis of strategies for resolving the conflict facing the team, the team leader planned her strategy. Prior to using the problem-solving technique, the team leader discussed with team members a procedure to address the issue before them. By doing so, she was seeking their cooperation and setting a climate so the issue might be resolved successfully.

Step One - Clarifying the problem

The task facing the team began with each side identifying its position on this issue.

- Team members K and L indicated their position was that the team should plan and teach a seven-day interdisciplinary unit during the current school year on some topic agreeable to all team members

- Team members R and S stated their position that no interdisciplinary units should be attempted during the current school year.

Step Two - Identifying the needs of both groups

The team leader asked each group to describe its needs. The two groups listed their needs as follows.

Needs of team members K and L (desiring interdisciplinary)
- they believed that teaching an interdisciplinary unit on a topic such as the   environment would help students see an issue from all sides
- viewing all team members working collaboratively would be a good model for their students to experience
- a feeling that this type of activity would help the team live up to the school's commitment when the middle school was established

Needs of team members R and S (opposing the unit)
- the apparent exorbitant amount of planning time to create such a unit would impinge on an already full schedule
- the time required to do such a unit would jeopardize their completion of the expected curriculum in their disciplines

Step Three - Restating their concern

After looking at the needs of fellow team members, the team leader asked both groups to try to restate the question attending to both group's needs. The statement they agreed to was this: *How can this team help students see connections in the curriculum without detracting from existing curricular expectations?* Both groups agreed that restating the issue did not commit either side to a specific means of achieving the goal but rather that each would make a sincere attempt to resolve this issue in a friendly and collaborative manner.

Step Four - Entering a consensus decision-making procedure.

The first step identified by the team leader was to brainstorm procedures that might result in helping students see connections in the curriculum. In a brainstorming session, the team members derived the following ideas.

- Reading a story in language arts that paralleled a topic in one of the other disciplines
- Having new vocabulary words from all the disciplines taught by the language arts teacher
- Mapping a timeline for the remainder of the year depicting major topics to be taught by each discipline represented on the team
- Having a teacher exchange day when teachers would teach topics in one another's classes
- Building an interdisciplinary unit around a field trip that had been taken in previous years and was planned again for this year
- Determining short units – two to three days – where similar complementary topics were taught in two or more disciplines
- Developing a short unit around a learning skill such as problem solving that was perceived as needed by students
- Having the language arts teacher work with other team members who are having students research and write reports
- Finding a unit developed by teachers in another school that would reduce the time needed to develop the unit
- Asking for time during an upcoming inservice day to develop an interdisciplinary unit that would meet their needs
- Asking for substitutes for all team members on a given day to plan an interdisciplinary unit
- Drawing on the professional resources that provide interdisciplinary units

At the conclusion of the brainstorming session, the team selected items E, J, and K. Ultimately it was decided that inservice time to plan an interdisciplinary unit around the field trip was agreeable and supportable by all.

Had the team failed to resolve the conflict, the team leader would then ask each side to try to work with her to reach a compromise. It was apparent that team members R and S felt they were under great pressure to complete their curriculum and did not feel they could delete seven days from their curriculum to teach an interdisciplinary unit. Team members K and L wanted the entire team to do something during the current year since the idea has been postponed for two years. The team leader could ask each side for some concessions that would have the least negative effect on its stated position.

SUMMARY

Conflict can be constructive or destructive. When teams encounter issues that result in differing opinions, it is important that the team and especially the team leader be aware of procedures for resolving the conflict. Each time a conflict is resolved successfully the team becomes stronger, more able to take risks and settle difficult issues in a successful manner.

However, if conflicts are to be resolved by a team, the following conditions must exist:

- Both parties must recognize that a problem exists and must be clear about the opposition's needs. It is helpful if each party can place itself in their opponent's shoes in order to gain a clearer understanding of their concerns.
- Be willing to discuss problems in a professional manner. This means active listening by both sides with special concern for hearing the other party's needs.
- A desire to work hard toward a resolution that will mutually benefit both parties. If the attitude is one of gaining more than one gives, the chance for reaching an agreement is lessened considerably. ❏

12

Recognizing and Managing Dysfunctional Team Behavior

Most potential teams can become real teams, but not without taking risks involving conflict, trust, interdependence, and hard work.

– Jon Katzenbach and Douglas Smith

T eams will, from time to time, exhibit dysfunctional behaviors; and individual team members often will act in nonproductive ways. A healthy team recognizes inappropriate behaviors and takes steps to correct them. While individual members of the team need to be on the watch for symptoms of team problems, it is especially important for the team leader and the principal to be aware of these signs.

SYMPTOMS OF DYSFUNCTIONAL TEAMS

Dysfunctional behaviors generally cluster in four areas: team focus, team leadership, team communication, and team ground rules.

Focus

Chapter 5 identifies the two most important characteristics of effective teams: they have established clear goals, and they evidence a commitment to work toward achieving these goals. Lacking either of these characteristics severely handicaps team effectiveness. Symptoms indicating a lack of team focus include

- unclear, unrealistic, or nonexistent goals
- no specific written agenda for team meetings
- no evidence of a commitment to the concept of teaming or a tapering off of the commitment

- reduction in the quality of the collaborative work of the team
- lack of consistency in production with shortcuts sometimes taken
- reports often late
- inadequate preparation for meetings
- inability to reach closure on any issue
- lack of creativity in team planning

Leadership

As detailed in Chapter 6, the team leader's role has not been clearly defined in many middle schools. Nonproductive team leader behaviors inevitably cause team dysfunction. Furthermore, as indicated in Chapter 7, a middle school principal who does not understand her/his role relative to interdisciplinary teams may also contribute to ineffective team behaviors.

Poor team leadership can cause the following dysfunctional behaviors:
- disorganized meetings that waste time
- no movement toward goals
- inability to make decisions, solve problems, or manage conflict
- unwillingness to take risks
- negative feelings toward teaming expressed both verbally and non-verbally
- confusion over responsibilities

Communication

For teams to be truly effective, there must be open communication between team members, with the team leader, between teams, and with the administration. Teams with communication problems likely show the following symptoms:
- hesitancy when speaking
- hiding true feelings
- blaming others for team problems
- forming cliques and alliances
- hidden agendas
- failing to share information with team members
- a major increase or decrease in verbal communication in meetings
- name calling and stereotyping

Ground rules

The behavior of team members is governed by rules or ground rules. Failure to establish these procedures can result in many difficulties. Teams that have not established ground rules or ignore them exhibit these dysfunctional behaviors:

- no exact starting and ending time
- absenteeism from meetings for trivial reasons
- interruptions of meetings
- no decision-making techniques for resolving difficult issues
- individuals do not adhere to team decisions
- lack of procedures to solve difficult problems
- decisions made with insufficient and/or unreliable information
- decisions made hurriedly and carelessly
- lack of trust of one another
- lack of respect for some members evident
- defensiveness and rancor occur when there is disagreement
- lack of patience
- unwillingness to cooperate with one another
- negative and critical behavior displayed by some members
- inadequate support for team members

MANAGING DYSFUNCTIONAL TEAMS

It would be wonderful if, for every dysfunctional behavior of teams or team members, specific procedures were available to remedy the situation. Dealing with these behaviors is similar to working with students who are having difficulties. While a general procedure may work with most students, each student's misbehavior must be treated as an individual situation. The same is true with team members and with teams that are not performing up to expectations. The general procedures that follow will suggest to teams, team leaders, and principals ways of helping individuals become effective team members, but the dynamics of the particular situation will require adjustments.

The team

Effective teams will find gentle ways to remind their members when they have broken ground rules Team-designed sanctions serve as friendly reminders to change one's behavior. Teams have adopted sanctions similar to the following:
- bringing refreshments to the next meeting
- placing a small fine into the team's social fund
- calling time when one individual has been speaking for a long period of time
- accepting any assignment given while absent without a valid reason

These sanctions serve more as reminders than punishment but do keep the team from becoming dysfunctional.

Discussing the offending behavior as a team is helpful. For example, if more than one member is late for team meetings, the team should revisit the ground rule. The team may decide to change the starting time or help one another find ways to be prompt.

The team leader

Dealing with an issue in which several team members have been guilty of transgressions is much easier than when the offense involves one individual. Teams that have a problem-solving technique for handling curricular or instructional issues can use this procedure for transgressions against team rules.

A strong team leader knows how to help a team resolve problems using such techniques as the following:

- support the team in invoking a sanction that was previously identified by the team
- review ground rules with the team when there are transgressions to these team-established procedures
- structure the meeting so all members will be involved in the discussion to prevent dominance by one or more members and nonparticipation by others
- structure a project to involve all members
- devise an agenda with limited time allocated to each item
- talk privately to the person whose behavior is a problem

If the team leader is not able to resolve a problem, assistance can be sought from other team leaders who may have dealt with a comparable problem. The team leader can also discuss the issue with the principal. Comments on the principal's role follows.

The principal

The principal plays an important role in handling ineffective team behaviors. First, the principal must make sure teams understand dysfunctional team behaviors. Small items such as coming late to meetings may be a way of life in a building, and arriving late for a team meeting is not seen as a problem. Helping team members understand and accept the concept of a "team" and those activities that will detract from the team's effective performance falls on the shoulders of the principal. Second, the principal must empower the team to solve its own problems by encouraging team members to deal directly with the problems and/or working with the team leader to resolve the issues. Third, everyone must understand that properly functioning teams are the expectation and the principal will take whatever action is necessary to ensure they do so. Fourth, it may be valuable for the principal to share with team members the cost associated with teaming. Calculating the cost to the district of one team meeting is an excellent means of reminding team members of their accountability to the district.

When the team cannot resolve the problem, the principal must intervene. This can be done in a number of ways:

- meet with the entire team to discuss the situation and make recommendations directly to the team
- deal separately with the person causing the problem. If the problem is severe, use such school district procedures as official reprimands
- reconstitute the team by changing team members
- assist the dysfunctional team member to find a non-team position in another school within the district
- assist the ineffective team member in find another position

While some of these actions are severe, the principal cannot tolerate dysfunctional teams or ineffective team members, for they impact directly on the welfare and achievement of students.

SUMMARY

Teams must be aware of the fact that some team conflict is normal and even positive, but if left alone, conflicts can become disabling. The team leader and principal must continuously monitor the progress of the team and the behavior of individual members to ensure early detection of problems. Knowing when to intercede and how to help members resolve their differences is an important role of the team leader. A team that can resolve conflicts will be a highly productive team. Chapter 11 provides some information on the management of conflict on teams as well as some ideas on conflict resolution. ❏

13

Teaming and Advisory Programs

These feelings of uncertainty and confusion in students demand that all aspects of the middle school program contribute to every student's personal growth and development. – Neila A. Connors

The primary goal of a middle school is to meet the physical, intellectual, social, and emotional needs of young adolescents. In many middle schools, the advisory program, often labeled teacher-advisor or advisor-advisee, has taken on the major responsibility for the social and emotional needs. Cole (1992) indicates "a teacher advisor program makes it possible for students to belong, meets their need to affiliate with a group, and makes caring manageable for a teacher, enabling the teacher to express concern in a personally satisfying way to a small number of individuals" (p. 7). In *Turning Points 2000* (Jackson & Davis, 2000) the authors point out "When they are done well, small-group advisories drawn from within the team provide a further opportunity for the personalized guidance and active monitoring young adolescents need" (p. 143).

However, Paul George and William Alexander (1993) say: "The advisor-advisee program is possibly the most attractive part of the entire middle school concept, but it seems to be the most difficult to implement successfully and carry out effectively over a period of years. Even after two decades of experience, in the 1990s many middle schools have begun with such programs only to find the idea scrapped after a year, sometimes in several months or even weeks" (pp. 224-225).

Why, then, does a program of such enormous potential for meeting the needs of students have such difficulty? According to Cole (1992), five of the most common reasons teacher-advisor programs fail to thrive are

- Insufficient planning time before beginning the program
- Inadequate preparation of teachers
- Incomplete development of topics and activities for the teacher advisory program
- Too frequent or too infrequent meetings of teacher-advisor groups
- Lack of administrative and/or counselor support for the program

It is somewhat ironic that while considerable time, effort, and money are devoted to the concept of teachers working together on teams in a middle school, usually each teacher in an advisory program functions independently. This need not be the case if a strategy is developed to weave together these two important middle school components. This chapter explores ways teaming and the advisory concept can be merged.

INTEGRATING TEAMING AND ADVISORY PROGRAMS

To implement this integrated model, three conditions must exist. First, the middle school must have a teaming program with approximately 25 students per teacher on the team. Second, the school must have allocated a 20-30 minute daily activity period to each team to meet with its students for a variety of experiences. Third, all students and only those students on the team are assigned to the team activity groups directed by the teachers on the team.

To move away from the traditional concept of a somewhat isolated advisory program, this 20-30 minute period allocated to each team will be labeled the team activity period. During this period, each team member is assigned approximately 25 students for whom this time becomes their homebase. Students report to this team member for selected activities and emigrate from this homebase to other activities offered during this time period.

In most middle schools, interdisciplinary teams focus on meeting the academic needs of students while the advisory program concentrates more on the personal, social, and emotional needs. In the proposed model, all students' needs are the responsibility of team members with attention to those needs provided through teaming activities and what takes place in the team activity period.

This model requires teams to develop a comprehensive plan to meet the physical, social, emotional, and intellectual needs of their students. Some of these needs will be augmented by other opportunities in the middle school such as the physical education program and guidance services. Teams must challenge themselves to utilize time and opportunities to meet as many student needs as possible. Since teams develop plans for their students independently, differences between team plans may exist. Differences allow team members to capitalize on their interests and strengths.

Intellectual needs

The disciplines represented on the team focus heavily on content, most of which is aimed at meeting the intellectual needs of students. In addition, embedded in the instruction is an emphasis on learning skills such as reading, writing, speaking, listening, decision making, problem solving, critical thinking, and information retrieval. While some learning skills are developed extensively in certain courses, they are the responsibility of all team members. Being aware of one another's curriculum, team members can cooperatively plan strategies to teach those skills across the curriculum. When that is done effectively, students see the connections in the curriculum that serve to reinforce mastering these skills.

Many learning skills can be enhanced by experiences in the activity period. Sustained silent reading and clubs, such as Olympics of the Mind, that stress thinking and problem solving extend and reinforce what has been taught by the academic team. Meeting with small groups for remedial work, offering accelerated academic-oriented activities for select groups of students, developing team projects related to their classwork, and involvement in service projects are examples of instructional activities that can be extended into the activity period.

Affective needs

A variety of strategies can be used to meet students' affective needs. Several are described below.

- Curriculum content
  Inevitably, some of the content of the basic disciplines will focus on issues related to students' affective needs. Team members should examine the curriculum to determine areas where academic content and social and emotional issues are connected. Some examples include
  Science – genetic engineering, environmental issues
  Social Studies – war, peace, hunger, divorce, cultural diversity, family changes, independence
  Language arts – feelings of empathy, self-worth, confidence, and accepting responsibility

  Making a direct connection between the social and emotional needs of young adolescents and the regular curriculum will increase the impact of these issues on students.

- Topics discussed in the team activity period
  Affective topics not covered in the regular curriculum can be placed in the team activity curriculum. Below are some topics that might be designated for inclusion in the activity period.
  understanding myself
  developing a positive self-concept
  career education
  school regulations
  transition into the middle school
  transition into the high school

  The amount of time allocated to these topics may depend on the grade level. For example, sixth grade students may focus heavily on transition into the middle school while grade eight may concentrate on the transition into the high school. When team members determine a need for providing instruction on a social or emotional topic such as bullying, the activity period provides the opportunity for it to take place.

- Student activities
  Because a number of students are not able to participate in after school activities, using the team activity period for clubs opens up opportunities for all students. Some clubs are natural extensions of a discipline, e.g., science club, poetry club, computer club. Others such as the student council and intramural activities can enrich the lives of middle level students. Finally, clubs may simply be a sharing of a teacher's special interest or hobby with students.

- Small group discussions
  The literature of advisory program recommends one teacher interacting with a small group of students. Serving as their advocate, this adult gets to know these students very well and the students in turn are able to turn to this adult in time of need. The very nature of the teaming program creates the opportunity for a small group of teachers getting to know and understand a small group of students. Likewise the students get to know their team teachers quite well. In the integrated model, a teacher, having 25 students assigned to a team activity  period, can split the group into two allowing the teacher the opportunity to meet with a smaller group. Those students not involved in the small group activity are reassigned for that day to other team members. Using this procedure during the course of the school year provides ample opportunity for one teacher to interact with a small group of students on an intimate basis. Small group activities can be scheduled at the discretion of the team.

- Personalized education plan for students

  A superb activity that meets many social and emotional needs of students as well as contributes to their intellectual needs is the development of a personalized education plan for each student on the team. The plan, developed by students with the help of a teacher, establishes a set of long- and short-term goals, strategies to achieve those goals, and a process to monitor and assess the goals. Student-led parent-teacher conferences involving portfolios to demonstrate student work serve as a capstone to this procedure. Most of these procedures would take place during the team activity period. Furthermore, a personalized education plan provides a continuous thread throughout the school year around which many team activity period activities can focus. Serving as an extension of the academic program, this provides a formal opportunity for one-to-one interaction between a teacher and a student.

POSITIVE ASPECTS OF THIS MERGER

By integrating the components of teaming and advisory into an inclusive unit, a number of advantages to students and teachers result.

- One of the major reasons for the difficulties advisory programs face is that many teachers do not feel comfortable addressing the kinds of topics that inevitably arise in advisory programs. During team planning time, these concerns can be expressed and plans made accordingly. For example, one person on the team could specialize in a particularly sensitive or difficult topic like alcoholism, and, over a period of days, meet with all students on the team during the team activity period to provide leadership in exploring this important topic.

- By working together, team members will not feel so isolated when interacting with students on social and emotional issues. Team members can support one another especially by sharing their strengths when dealing with personal growth concerns. There is time to collectively plan activities during the team planning time thus reducing the sense of isolation prevalent with most advisory programs.
- The linking provides connections between the academic work and social and emotional activities.
- Team members bring their extensive knowledge of students to the team activity period.
- Small groups can be formed when team members cooperate with one another. Likewise, large groups can be formed since all students in the team activity period belong to one team. Speakers and videos on topics such as drugs or sexual harassment can reach all students in an efficient manner that can be followed up in small group discussions.
- In this model, encore or exploratory teachers are not assigned a team activity group. Encore teachers could, on occasions, support the core team efforts by assisting with special activities. In a middle school with a large number of encore teachers, they could be divided into groups and assigned to supplement the work of each team. Furthermore, they could supervise scarce resources such as a computer laboratory made available to students during the activity time period.
- Since all students on a team are under the jurisdiction of the core teachers during the activity period, this becomes an ideal time for the encore teachers to meet as a team one or more days each week.

SUMMARY

The move to meld the teaming and advisory programs is in keeping with the middle school advocacy of curriculum integration. This model can be a powerful strategy for meeting the diverse needs of students. Some of the concerns that accompany advisory programs can be alleviated by this proposal. The power of teaming can be applied positively to the advisory component, a component that has been difficult to implement. ❑

14

Assessment Instruments

Smell the cheese often so you know
when it is getting old.

– Spencer Johnson

Teaming is a vehicle to assist teachers in providing a quality teaching and learning experience for students. As with all vehicles, it is important to have periodic checkups to determine the vehicle's effectiveness. The instruments contained in this chapter are provided as assessment tools to assist in the journey toward developing high performance teams. How, when, and to whom they will be administered as well as how the responses will be utilized are matters that will need to be decided in a particular school.

The items contained in this instrument represent expectations of quality teaming described in the middle school literature on teaming. After being validated by nationally recognized experts on teaming, the instrument was pilot tested and utilized by a number of middle schools to assess teaming effectiveness. Slightly altered versions are provided for parent and student perceptions of teaming. In addition a Team Leader Checklist, a Principal Effectiveness Instrument, a Team Conflict Inventory, and a Team Progress Survey are provided. These instruments can and should be adapted to fit particular situations

STAFF ASSESSMENT OF TEAMING

Directions: For each item, indicate the degree to which the factor is characteristic of teaming in your middle level school.

A. Significant degree
B. Moderate degree
C. Slight degree
D. Not at all
E. Do not know

Team planning

In our middle level school...

_____ 1. team responsibilities are clearly defined

_____ 2. each team member has some specific and defined responsibilities

_____ 3. all team members fulfill their role responsibilities

_____ 4. teams have the authority to make decisions

_____ 5. teams are skilled in decision-making procedures needed when addressing difficult situations

_____ 6. all team members participate in team decisions

_____ 7. every member supports decisions made

_____ 8. records are kept of all team decisions, activities, and student information

_____ 9. team members use common planning time effectively

_____ 10. team meetings follow a prepared agenda

_____ 11. team members are open and honest with one another

_____ 12. the location and setting of team meetings are conducive to effective team work

_____ 13. a team calendar is maintained so items such as exams and special assignments can be coordinated

_____ 14. team members support the team leader

_____ 15. all team members take turns at leadership tasks

_____ 16. the team has a budget for discretionary items

_____ 17. the teaming arrangement empowers teachers to be participants in the school's decision-making process

_____ 18. there is a sense of purpose evident in each team

_____ 19. team members display a commitment to the teaming process

_____ 20. teams use planning time to discuss middle level issues including curriculum

_____ 21. team members are capable of building consensus

_____ 22. teams conduct team meetings with students present and participating when appropriate

Communication

In our middle level school...

_____ 23. team members communicate effectively with guidance counselors

_____ 24. team members communicate effectively with media center persons

_____ 25. team members communicate effectively with the administration

_____ 26. team members communicate effectively with special education personnel

_____ 27. team members communicate effectively with teachers who are not team members

_____ 28. team members communicate effectively with parents of students on their team

_____ 29. team members communicate effectively with students on their team

_____ 30. teams communicate effectively with other teams

Curriculum and instruction

In our middle level school...

_____ 31. team members organize curriculum and instruction to achieve team goals

_____ 32. attempts are made to structure the curriculum so that team members teach related topics at the same time

_____ 33. team members find multiple ways to connect and relate the disciplines represented on the team

_____ 34. team members find multiple ways to involve various subject areas not represented on the team

_____ 35. learning skills taught in one class are reinforced by other team members

_____ 36. team members discuss curricular issues on a regular basis

_____ 37. the team utilizes the opportunities inherent in block scheduling by altering time allotment and group sizes

_____ 38. teaming has made it possible to effect changes in the curriculum

_____ 39. teaming has made it easier to effect changes in instructional procedures

_____ 40. team members feel they are more effective teachers because they are part of a team

Interpersonal relationships

In our middle level school...

_____ 41. team members cooperate with one another

_____ 42. team members support each other

_____ 43. team members seek to learn from one another

_____ 44. there is a sense of professionalism among team members

_____ 45. there is a spirit of cooperation between teams within the school

_____ 46. experienced team members provide help and support to new team members

_____ 47. team members provide assistance to substitute teachers

_____ 48. team members provide quality learning opportunities for student teachers

_____ 49. team members willingly subject themselves to professional evaluation

_____ 50. team members utilize the strengths of each other

_____ 51. team members provide feedback to one another

_____ 52. team members are knowledgeable about group dynamics

_____ 53. team members are knowledgeable of conflict resolution procedures and use them

_____ 54. team members work to develop a team identity

_____ 55. team members manage stressful situations

_____ 56. team members actively listen to one another

Team functions

In our middle level school...

_____ 57. teams hold conferences with students when appropriate

_____ 58. teams hold conferences with parents when appropriate

_____ 59. team members coordinate assignments for the benefit of students

_____ 60. teams set and work toward yearly goals

_____ 61. teams conduct self-evaluation of their goals and functions

_____ 62. teams group and regroup students

_____ 63. teams have a consistent set of behavioral expectations for students

_____ 64. teams have a consistent set of academic expectations for students

_____ 65. team members are consistent in their disciplinary techniques
_____ 66. teams use community resources
_____ 67. teams incorporate instructional aids in their teaching
_____ 68. team members discuss teaching strategies
_____ 69. teams include non-team staff members in deliberations regarding student progress and/or behavior
_____ 70. teams provide regular progress reports to parents beyond the district-wide report card

Effects on students

In our middle level school...

_____ 71. each student appears to relate well to at least one team member
_____ 72. team members respond to each student's social and emotional growth
_____ 73. team members are aware of each student's cognitive needs
_____ 74. team members provide recognition for all students on the team
_____ 75. team members develop social activities for students on the team
_____ 76. team members recognize special needs and talents of students on the team
_____ 77. teams plan special events for students
_____ 78. student disciplinary referrals are minimal

Public relations

In our middle level school...

_____ 79. teams provide special events for parents of students on their team
_____ 80. team members are strong advocates of the interdisciplinary organization
_____ 81. teaming is supported by the administration of the school
_____ 82. teaming is supported by the Board of Education
_____ 83. team members share information about team activities with the community
_____ 84. teaming is supported by the parents of students
_____ 85. teaming receives support by the news media

PARENT ASSESSMENT OF TEAMING

Directions: For each item, please indicate the degree to which the factor is characteristic of teaming in your child's middle level school.

      A. Significant degree
      B. Moderate degree
      C. Slight degree
      D. Not at all
      E. Do not know

In our middle level school...

_____ 1. team members communicate effectively with teachers who are not team members

_____ 2. team members communicate effectively with parents of students on their team

_____ 3. team members communicate effectively with students on their team

_____ 4. attempts are made to structure the curriculum so team members teach related topics at the same time

_____ 5. learning skills, initially taught in one class, are reinforced by other team members

_____ 6. team members support each other

_____ 7. there is a sense of professionalism evident among team members

_____ 8. there is a spirit of cooperation between teams within the school

_____ 9. teams hold conferences with students when appropriate

_____ 10. teams conference with parents when appropriate

_____ 11. team members coordinate assignments for the benefit of students

_____ 12. teams hold conferences with parents when necessary beyond those regularly scheduled by the school

_____ 13. teams have and communicate to parents a consistent set of behavioral expectations for their students

_____ 14. teams have and communicate to parents a consistent set of academic expectations for their students

_____ 15. team members are consistent in applying their disciplinary techniques

_____ 16. team makes considerable use of community resources

_____ 17. teams include other staff members in deliberations regarding student progress and behavior

_____ 18. teams provide regular progress reports to parents

_____ 19. every student relates well to at least one team member

_____ 20. team members respond to each student's social and emotional growth

_____ 21. team members recognize each student's intellectual needs

_____ 22. team members provide recognition for all students on the team

_____ 23. team members develop social activities for students on the team

_____ 24. team members recognize special needs and talents of students on the team

_____ 25. teams plan special events for students

_____ 26. teams provide special events for parents of students on their team

_____ 27. team members are strong advocates of teaming

_____ 28. teaming is supported by the administration of the school

_____ 29. teaming is supported by the Board of Education

_____ 30. teaming is supported by the parents of students in the school

STUDENT ASSESSMENT OF TEAMING

Directions: For each item please indicate the degree to which you believe the statement is characteristic of teaming in your middle level school.

        A. Significant degree
        B. Moderate degree
        C. Slight degree
        D. Not at all
        E. Do not know

In our middle level school ...

_____ 1. teachers communicate effectively with students on their team

_____ 2. attempts are made by teachers to teach related topics at the same time

_____ 3. skills learned in one class are used in other classes

_____ 4. a spirit of cooperation exists among the teachers on the team

_____ 5. a spirit of cooperation between teams within the school exists

_____ 6. students feel good about the team to which they are assigned

_____ 7. teams conference with students when appropriate

_____ 8. teachers avoid giving major assignments and tests on the same day

_____ 9. students can be switched to different classes within the team

_____ 10. teachers on the team have the same rules and regulations for all students

_____ 11. teachers on the team discipline students in the same way

_____ 12. teachers talk with other teachers in the school about students who are on the team

_____ 13. each student is able to get to know at least one of their teachers on the team very well

_____ 14. teachers recognize students for outstanding performance

_____ 15. teachers develop social activities for students on the team

_____ 16. teachers plan special events for students on their team

TEAM LEADER CHECKLIST

This checklist identifies team leader expectations for highly effective teams. For each item, indicate the extent to which you believe perform this role as the team leader.

        A. Significant degree
        B. Moderate degree
        C. Slight degree
        D. Not at all

Vision

As team leader, I...

_____ 1. share my beliefs in the power of teaming
_____ 2. share new ideas with my team
_____ 3. challenge my team to take risks
_____ 4. challenge my team to more effectively improve student learning

Leadership

As team leader, I...

_____ 5. assist the team in establishing effective decision-making procedures for difficult and important decisions
_____ 6. utilize the team's established decision-making procedures when difficult and important decisions must be made
_____ 7. assist the team in establishing an effective problem-solving procedure for difficult and important problems
_____ 8. utilize the team's established problem-solving procedures when difficult and important problems must be made
_____ 9. help the team understand the sources of conflict for teams
_____ 10. help the team understand how conflict can be both constructive and destructive
_____ 11. assist the team in understanding procedures to prevent conflict on the team
_____ 12. assist the team in establishing conflict resolution procedures
_____ 13. utilize the team's established conflict resolution procedures when conflicts need resolution

_____ 14. understand and am sensitive to the feelings and behaviors of team members inherent in each stage of team development

_____ 15. am able to diagnose the developmental stage of the team

_____ 16. provide appropriate leadership for the team at each stage of development

_____ 17. utilize a variety of decision-making styles

_____ 18. am aware of the particular strengths of each team member

_____ 19. am aware of the particular concerns of each team member

Team functioning

As team leader, I...

_____ 20. assist the team in establishing general goals

_____ 21. assist the team in establishing measurable goals

_____ 22. help the team define team member's roles

_____ 23. ensure appropriate team record keeping activities

_____ 24. assist with the development of basic ground rules

_____ 25. encourage team members to maintain established ground rules

_____ 26. prepare an agenda for each team meeting

_____ 27. keep the meeting focused on the agenda items

_____ 28. discourage interruptions to team meetings

_____ 29. assist the team to set common classroom management and instructional expectations for students

_____ 30. assist the team in capitalizing on connections among the various subjects

_____ 31. seek necessary resources for the team

Team climate

As team leader, I...

_____ 32. encourage team members to develop and support a positive team climate

_____ 33. help the team to find ways to celebrate student and team successes

_____ 34. assist the team in developing trusting relationships

_____ 35. give special attention and support to new team members

Communication

As team leader, I...

_____ 36. communicate openly and honestly with team members

_____ 37. confront the team on critical issues

_____ 38. assist the team to communicate with other teams and personnel in the school

_____ 39. provide assistance to individual team members when they are experiencing difficulties

_____ 40. assist the team in being sensitive to the impact of verbal and non-verbal behaviors

Assessment

As team leader, I...

_____ 41. assist the team in continuously evaluating its effectiveness

_____ 42. am willing to seek assistance in dealing with difficult team situations

Personal competence

As team leader, I...

_____ 43. understand the nature of middle school students

_____ 44. understand and espouse the middle school philosophy

_____ 45. incorporate technology into the instructional activities

_____ 46. utilize a variety of instructional strategies in the classroom

_____ 47. utilize effective classroom management skills in the classroom

_____ 48. participate in staff development opportunities to improve the teaching abilities

_____ 49. demonstrate an interest in cross-curricular connections

PRINCIPAL EFFECTIVENESS INSTRUMENT

This checklist identifies expectations for principals in middle schools with highly effective teams. For each item, indicate the extent to which you believe you perform this role as principal.

        A. Significant degree
        B. Moderate degree
        C. Slight degree
        D. Not at all

As principal, I...

_____ 1. believe that teaming is an effective organizational structure for the middle school

_____ 2. understand the concept of teaming and the opportunities it provides for teachers and students.

_____ 3. share my expectations of teaming with all personnel in the middle school

_____ 4. share my understandings and expectations of teaming with appropriate personnel in the school district

_____ 5. am comfortable selecting new teachers to work on teams

_____ 6. am able to appropriately place teachers on teams

_____ 7. monitor team leaders by attending team meetings

_____ 8. monitor the team's work by viewing student activities

_____ 9. am aware of individual team member performance

_____ 10. make personnel changes in the composition of teams when necessary

_____ 11. encourage and assist in the professional development of teams

_____ 12. am knowledgeable about the stages of team development

_____ 13. am aware of each team's stage of development

_____ 14. require teams to establish challenging and measurable goals

_____ 15. require periodic team reports on the progress toward achieving their goals

_____ 16. require weekly reports on team activities

_____ 17. provide a written response to weekly team leader reports

_____ 18. provide teams with a meeting room with appropriate accessories where possible

_____ 19. provide teams with a discretionary budget to support team activities

_____ 20. praise and rewards teams for their achievements

_____ 21. place all teachers in my building on teams

_____ 21. developed a job description for team leaders

_____ 23. developed a process for selecting quality team leaders

_____ 24. am responsible for the final selection of team leaders

_____ 25. meet with team leaders on a weekly or biweekly basis

_____ 26. provide training for team leaders

_____ 27. developed a tenure plan for team leaders

_____ 28. provide appropriate positive reinforcement to team leaders

_____ 29. provide assistance to team leaders to help their teams with solving problems when needed

_____ 30. encourage teams to make their own decisions, solve their own problems, and manage conflicts

_____ 31. assist team leaders in assessing their progress as team leaders

TEAM CONFLICT INVENTORY

The following items represent potential sources of destructive conflict in interdisciplinary teams. Responses to these items can assist teams in rectifying issues before they become major dilemmas.

Use the following scale to have each team member rate your team's potential for conflict development.

A. Agree completely

B. Agree

C. Disagree

D. Disagree completely

Team focus

_____ 1. Team goals are clear to all team members
_____ 2. Team goals relate to student achievement
_____ 3. Team goals reflect student social and emotional needs
_____ 4. Team goals are reviewed on a regular basis
_____ 5. Data are collected and discussions held on a regular basis to determine progress on team goals
_____ 6. There is a written agenda for each team meeting
_____ 7. The team agenda guides the conduct of the team meeting
_____ 8. Team members control their own agenda not allowing other personnel in the school to dictate the agenda to them

Sharing the team workload

_____ 9. Each member of the team has a specific role or roles to perform
_____ 10. Each member fulfills the responsibility of the assigned role

Team leadership

_____ 11. There is a designated team leader
_____ 12. The team leader prepares a written agenda for each meeting
_____ 13. The team leader has received leadership training
_____ 14. A team leader job description exists
_____ 15. The team leader utilizes a variety of leadership styles
_____ 16. The team leader communicates effectively with team members

Communication

_____ 17. Team members refrain from put-downs or stereotyping
_____ 18. Team members feel free to speak on any topic
_____ 19. Team members listen attentively and openly to all ideas
_____ 20. Team members utilize appropriate nonverbal behaviors
_____ 21. Team members can express their viewpoint without being interrupted
_____ 22. Team members refrain from side conversations
_____ 23. Team members do not have hidden personal agendas
_____ 24. Team conversations are not dominated by one or two people
_____ 25. All team members contribute to team discussions

Team ground rules

_____ 26. Team meetings start and end at designated times

_____ 27. Team meetings are not interrupted except for emergencies

_____ 28. All team members attend all team meetings

Team decision making, problem solving, and conflict management

_____ 29. A problem-solving process exists for addressing difficult and important decisions

_____ 30. Team members are able to make difficult decisions that all members can support

_____ 31. Team members adhere to team decisions

_____ 32. Team members are skilled in using a procedure to solve difficult problems

_____ 33. A conflict resolution procedure exists for resolving difficult conflicts and is used successfully.

TEAM PROGRESS SURVEY

These three questions can be used to comprise an open-ended survey. They will help teams initiate discussion on their teaming progress. Their use is especially effective shortly after teams have been in operation but can be used on a yearly or other basis.

1. What positive accomplishments can be attributed to your team? Address accomplishments as they relate to students, staff, parents, curriculum, instruction, etc. Be as specific as possible and provide any evidence you have for these accomplishments.

2. What aspects of teaming have you not accomplished? Address these items as they relate to students, staff, parents, curriculum, instruction, etc. Be as specific as possible and indicate the reason(s) they have not been accomplished.

3. What resources does your team need to accomplish the tasks desired by the team? Resources may be in the form of staff development, budget, time, facilities, equipment, support, etc. ❏

15

Resources

The resources in Chapter 15 support the ideas presented in previous chapters. Contents of this chapter include

- Suggested readings
  The materials in this section will give the readers sources to peruse to gain additional information on topics addressed in this book.

- Team celebration ideas
  When something positive has been accomplished by team members or students on the team, celebrations are in order. The celebration ideas presented in this chapter were collected from middle school team members.

- Forms for developing consistent management and instructional procedures for teams.
  Used with the initial development of teams, these forms have proven beneficial as teams attempt to establish consistent classroom management and instructional practices.

- Individual/team technology profile
  Completing this profile will help individuals and teams assess their technological competencies.

- References

SUGGESTED READING

Books

Bader, G. E., Bloom, A. E., & Chang, R. Y. (1994). *Measuring team performance*. Irvine, CA: Richard Chang Associates.

Blanchard, K. (1982). *Leadership and the one minute manager*. New York: William Morrow and Company, Inc.

Chang, R. Y. (1994). *Building a dynamic team*. Irvine, CA: Richard Chang Associates.

Dickinson, T. S., & Erb, T. O. (1997). *We gain more than we give: Teaming in middle schools*. Columbus, OH: National Middle School Association.

Fisher, R., & Ury, W. (1983). *Getting to yes: Negotiating agreement without giving in*. New York: Penguin Books.

Harrington-Mackin, D. (1994). *The team building tool kit: Tips, tactics, and rules for effective work place teams*. New York: American Management Association.

Kelly, P. K. (1994). *Team decision-making techniques*. Irvine, CA: Richard Chang Associates.

Klubnik, J. P., & Greenwood, P. F. (1994). *The team-based problem solver*. New York: Irwin Professional Publishing.

Lambert, L. (1998). *Building leadership capacity in schools*. Alexandria VA: Association for Supervision and Curriculum Development.

Lounsbury, J. H. (Ed.). (1992). *Connecting the curriculum through interdisciplinary instruction*. Columbus, OH: National Middle School Association.

Maddux, R. B. (1992). *Team building: an exercise in leadership*. Menlo Park, CA: Crisp Publication, Inc.

Maginn, Michael D. (1994). *Effective teamwork*. New York: Business One Irwin/Mirror Press.

McIntosh-Fletcher, D. (1996). *Teaming design by real teams for real people*. Chicago, IL: Irwin Professional Publishing.

Potter, B. (1996). *From conflict to cooperation: How to mediate a dispute*. Berkeley, CA: Ronin Publishing, inc.

Robbins, H., & Finley, M. (1995). *Why teams don't work. Princeton*, NJ: Peterson's Pacesetter Books.

Straub, J. T. (1998). *The agile manager's guide to building and leading teams*. Bristol, VT: Velocity Business Publishing.

Ury, W. (1991). *Getting past no: Negotiating with difficult people.* New York: Bantam Books.

Zander, A. (1994). *Making groups effective.* San Francisco: Jossey-Bass Publishers.

Articles

Bishop, P, & Stevenson, C. (2000). When smaller is greater: Two or three partner teams. *Middle School Journal, 31* (3), 12-17.

Rottier, J. (2000). The principal and teaming: Unleashing the power of collaboration. *Schools in the Middle, 5* (4), 31-36.

Rottier, J. (2000). Teaming in the middle school: Improve it or lose it. *The Clearing House, 73* (4), 214-216.

Smith, H. W. (1991) Guide to teaming development. *Middle School Journal, 22* (5), 21-23.

Trimble, S., and Rottier, J. (2000). Assessing team performance. *Schools in the Middle, 8* (3), 31-3

CELEBRATION ACTIVITIES FOR TEAMS

Food

Bagel day   Bring in lunch
Go out to lunch   Barbecue
Bread day   Breakfast
Cake and ice cream social   Restaurant certificates
Surprise luncheon   Wine and cheese at homes
Candy   Cookie exchange
Dinner out   Feed the teacher day
Food parties   Lunch provided by the school
Pop a bottle of champagne   Potluck

Social/recreational

Comedy club   Movie or play
Happy hour   Health resort
Shopping outing   Men's cigar club
Hot tub party   Karaokee night
Monthly coffee   Bowl, golf, volleyball
Poetry party   Pool party
White elephant groups   Share hobby day
Quilting bees   Share picture day
Attend sporting events   T.G.I.F.
Game night (e.g. Trivial Pursuit)

Dress

Dress alike   Dress down day
Dress up day   Funny hair day
Tasteful T-shirt day   Team uniforms
Costume day

Gifts

Gag gifts at Christmas   Birthday
Secret pals

Extra time

Get out early   No duties
No hall duty   Principal-in-class day
Time off

Trips

Off-site team day   Overnight retreat
Organized trips   Visit other schools
Conferences/workshops

Other

Media coverage   Miss a meeting day
Open house   Secret pals
Swap teachers day   Team picture
Awards/ceremony   Notes
Wall of fame   Share bright spots/success

CELEBRATION ACTIVITIES FOR STUDENTS

Extra time

Art activity-extra time   Free note writing time
Free reading   Get out early
Longer breaks   Quiet talk time

Assemblies/concerts

Attend concert / theater   Guest speakers
Clowns, magicians   Talent show

Awards

Certificates   Diversity celebration
Merit slips   Grade raising awards
Locker decorating   Media coverage
Non-food awards   Notes of appreciation
Pictures posted   Unique awards (bug award)
Team display   Take their picture
Good news letters to parents   Recognition in local newspaper

Food

Banana splits   Breakfast treat
Fast food coupons   Decorate cookies
Food- special lunch   Juice during class
Chew gum in class   Pizza party
Pop party   Popcorn party
Snacks- snack day   Snow cones
Staff/ student lunch   Suckers
Treats   Take student(s) out to lunch

Recreational/social

Beach party   Board game time
Carnival   Christmas caroling
Game day   Dance
Free time- gym, outdoors   Learning games
Overnight lock-in   Movie day
Olympics activities   Pool party
Room party   Scavenger hunt
Sing along   Skating party
Ski trip   Sledding
Snow sculpture contest   Students vs. staff activities
T-shirts Team recreation day   Team trivia contest
Team uniforms   Toy box day
Walk in park   Waterslide party
Work-free day   Team camp out
"Special" day (tie day, pajama day, pets, hats, etc.)

Visits

Field trip   Grandparents day
Parents day   Sibling day
Science museum   Visit the poor
Zoo   Pet day

Academic

Class outside   No grade day
No homework

Other

Movie

Balloon release

Homework free coupon

First in line for lunch

Funny hair day

Show and tell

Celebrate birthdays

Service projects

Lunch with principal

Lunch with teachers

Bike trip – parents and kids

Charitable contributions

Lunch outside

Fund raisers

Late assignment coupon

Buttons

Banners

Decorate door contest

Picnic with parents

CLASSROOM MANAGEMENT PROCEDURES FORMS

The Classroom Management Procedures Form is a guide for teams as they determine team procedures for classroom management concerns.

Classroom Management Procedures
"What's Best for Kids"

Item	Team Procedures
1. Tardiness	
2. Leaving the Classroom	
Lockers	
Bathroom	
Office	
Nurse	
Guidance office	
Water fountain	
3. Cheating	
Tests	
Daily work	

Item	Team Procedures

4. Positive Reinforcement
    Student recognition
    Birthdays
    Calls to parents
    Team activities	

5. Punishments
    Detention
    Loss of privileges
    Extra work
    Lowering academic marks	

6. Other
    Poor language
    Food in classroom
    Chewing gum
    Books not covered
    Notewriting
    Organizational notebook
    Required supplies
    Other	

The Classroom Instructional Procedures Form is a guide for teams as they determine team procedures for instructional concerns.

Classroom Instructional Procedures
"What's Best for Kids"

Item	Team Procedures
1. Evaluation Numerical/letter grades Grading scale Extra credit Late work Make-up work Proficiency reports Deficiency reports Grading adjustments (Special needs students) Other 2. Homework Frequency of assignments Length of assignments Evaluation of homework Percentage correct Based on effort Paper headings	

The Analysis of Learning Skills Chart provides a strucure for teams as they determine which learning skills are taught by each teacher on the team.

Skills	Reading	Writing	Listening	Speaking	Note Taking	Study Skills	Information Retrieval	Test Taking	Organization
Science									
Math									
Social Studies									
Language Arts									
Reading									
Art									
Music									
Family & Consumer Education									
Technology Education									
Physical Education									
Foreign Language									
Other									

Analysis of Learning Skills

The Teaming Learning Skills Analysis Chart serves as a guide for teams as they decide common procedures for teaching learning skills.

Team Learning Skills Analysis
"What's Best for Kids"

Item	Team Procedures
1. Reading	
2. Writing	
3. Listening	
4. Speaking	
5. Note Taking	
6. Study Skills	
7. Information Retrieval	
8. Thinking/Problem Solving	
9. Test Taking	
10. Organization	

Individual/Team Technology Profile

The purpose of this survey is to assess the computer competency level of team members and the team in order to determine technology training needs. For each competency, use the rating scale below to indicate the level of expertise of each team member by placing a check in the box under the appropriate rating.

1. Not familiar with this competency, have not used it
2. Familiar with the competency but have only begun to work with it
3. Quite comfortable with this competency
4 Very comfortable and able to teach this competency to others

Competencies   Rating

Basic computer competencies

Competency	1	2	3	4
Install a new software program	1	2	3	4
Use a word processing program	1	2	3	4
Create spreadsheets	1	2	3	4
Manage files (open, save, print, etc.)	1	2	3	4
Use a grading program	1	2	3	4
Create and use a database; print reports	1	2	3	4

Graphics/Multimedia

Competency	1	2	3	4
Use clip art	1	2	3	4
Create charts and graphs	1	2	3	4
Use desktop publishing (e.g., Pagemaker)	1	2	3	4
Utilize CD-ROM programs	1	2	3	4
Use presentation software (e.g., Powerpoint)	1	2	3	4
Use digital sound	1	2	3	4

Create integrated multimedia-combine elements from several applications	1	2	3	4
Use computer television projection equipment (e.g., In Focus)	1	2	3	4
Use computer overhead projection equipment	1	2	3	4
Use scanners and/or digital cameras	1	2	3	4
Use desktop video production (e.g., Avid Camera)	1	2	3	4

Other

Telecommunication

Send and receive electronic mail	1	2	3	4
Use electronic databases (e.g., Badger Link)	1	2	3	4
Use an electronic bulletin board	1	2	3	4
Use a web browser to access information	1	2	3	4
Set up web pages for instruction	1	2	3	4
Capable of teaching over interactive television	1	2	3	4
Use listservs to send and receive mail	1	2	3	4
Access and/or develop Webquests	1	2	3	4

Other

References

Carnegie Council on Adolescent Development. (1989). *Turning points: Preparing American youth for the 21st century.* New York: Carnegie Corporation.

Chang, R. (1994). *Success through teamwork.* Irvine, CA: Richard Chang Associates, Inc.

Cole, C. (1992). *Nurturing a teacher advisory program.* Columbus, OH: National Middle School Association.

Fisher, R., & Ury, W. (1983). *Getting to yes: Negotiating agreement without giving in.* New York: Penguin Books.

George, P., & Shewey, K. (1994). *New evidence for the middle school.* Columbus, OH: National Middle School Association.

George, P. S., & Alexander, W. M. (1993). *The exemplary middle school.* (2nd cd.). Fort Worth, TX: Harcourt Brace Jovanovich College Publishers.

Jackson, A., & Davis, G. (2000). *Turning points 2000.* New York: Teachers College Press.

Johnson, D., & Johnson, R. (1987). *Joining together.* Edgewood Cliffs, NJ: Prentice Hall.

Kayser, T. (1994). *Team power.* New York: Professional Publishing.

Maddux, R. (1992). *Team building: An exercise in leadership.* Menlo Park, CA: Crisp Publications, Inc.

Martin, D. (1991). *Team think.* New York: Penguin Books.

Raider, E. (1992). *Conflict resolution through collaborative negotiation.* New York: International Center for Cooperation and Conflict Resolution.

Rottier, J., Landon, G., & Rush, L. (1995). *The middle level schools in Wisconsin: Growth from 1989 to 1994.* Madison, WI: Wisconsin Department of Public Instruction.

Scholtes, P. R. (1992). *The team handbook: How to use teams to improve quality.* Madison, WI: Joiner Associates, Inc.

Tuckman, B. W. (1965). Developmental sequence in small groups. *Psychological Bulletin, 63* (6), 384-399.

Zander, A. (1994). *Making groups effective* (2nd ed.). San Francisco: Jossey Bass Publishers.